THE CITIZEN'S CHOICE

THE CITIZEN'S CHOICE

by

ERNEST BARKER

οὐχ ὑμᾶς δαίμων λήξεται, ἀλλ' ὑμεῖς δαίμονα
αἱρήσεσθε... αἰτία ἑλομένου.   PLATO

Essay Index Reprint Series

 BOOKS FOR LIBRARIES PRESS
FREEPORT, NEW YORK

First Published 1937
Reprinted 1972

Library of Congress Cataloging in Publication Data

Barker, Sir Ernest, 1874-1960.
  The citizen's choice.

  (Essay index reprint series)
  Reprint of the 1937 ed.
  CONTENTS: The conflict of ideologies.--The break-
down of democracy.--The social background of recent
political changes. [etc.]
    1. Political science--Addresses, essays, lectures.
2. Democracy--Addresses, essays, lectures. I. Title
JC257.B3 1972   320   72-300
ISBN 0-8369-2784-2

PRINTED IN THE UNITED STATES OF AMERICA
BY
NEW WORLD BOOK MANUFACTURING CO., INC.
HALLANDALE, FLORIDA 33009

CONTENTS

PREFACE

The papers collected in this little volume, under a title for which I have to thank the insight and the ingenuity of the Secretary of the Cambridge University Press, belong to a most stirring period in the history of human affairs. They were all composed in the years from 1933 to 1937, between the beginning of the National Socialist Revolution in Germany and the end (not yet in sight) of the Civil War in Spain. In a world perplexed by the problem of choice I have sought to consider the great alternatives. In a country which still follows the great tradition inaugurated in the seventeenth century—the tradition of Milton and Cromwell—I have tried to obey the teaching of my masters. I have remembered, even if I have not fulfilled, the noble injunction of Milton, 'to argue freely according to conscience'. I have remembered, even if I have sometimes failed to follow, the saying of Cromwell in Putney Church in the autumn of 1647: 'If we may come to an honest and single debate, how we may all agree in one common way for public good; if we meet so, we shall meet with a great deal the more comfort and hopes of a good and happy issue and understanding of the business. But if otherwise, I despair.'

It is in that spirit that I have attempted to contribute to the great debate of our days. I trust that I have not too much condemned or blamed any side or any cause. Perhaps I have gone to the other extreme, and have been too much detached and impersonal. I can only plead a deep sense that each country has its own speech, its own deep and incommunicable associations embedded in that speech, its own way of looking at the world. On the other hand, particularly in our days, common and general European currents of opinion are flowing over all countries alike. The result is an amalgam, peculiar in each country and peculiar to each country—an amalgam between its own way of life and the deposits of the common European currents. That amalgam has to be studied and understood, in each case, on its own merits. Yet there abides a single and permanent touchstone above all this relativity, a touchstone which is universal and common to all countries and nations—the touchstone which tests the quality of all human systems by the degree of their respect for the plain human dignity of the individual man. That is ultimate, and absolute. It is the final standard of judgment which every thinker who believes in a kingdom and power and glory above the nations, acting in and upon each individual human soul, must necessarily apply. If I have said little or nothing about that final standard in these essays, it is not from forgetfulness. It was always present in my mind. It is the basis of everything which I have written in this book.

ERNEST BARKER

CAMBRIDGE

August 1937

I

THE CONFLICT OF
IDEOLOGIES

Delivered at Chatham House, 16 March 1937

A lecture by a Professor! I apologise. But as Scott says somewhere, 'Even a haggis, God bless her, can charge downhill!' On such a subject as that of to-night, even a Professor, Heaven help him, may perhaps be interesting.

'The Conflict of Ideologies.' But what is an ideology? It is a barbarous term, popularised of late by our Foreign Minister, a boundless, formless, horrendous monster without any light, *monstrum horrendum informe ingens, cui lumen ademptum*. The word, so far as I know, has come to us from France; and in its original sense, which belongs to the end of the eighteenth century, it meant the science of ideas, or the philosophy of mind, and more especially that philosophy which derives our knowledge from the senses. Early in the nineteenth century, Napoleon seized the word, and twisting it to an opposite sense applied it as a nickname to the revolutionary scheme of abstract political metaphysics, or, as one might also call it, using a term current in Germany over a hundred years ago and adopted by Coleridge, 'metapolitics'. Sir Walter Scott said of Napoleon's use of the word ideology that it 'served him to distinguish every species of theory which, resting in no respect on the basis of self-interest, could prevail with none but hot-brained boys and crazed enthusiasts'. The word seems to have undergone a new change in the twentieth century. It has been adopted by the Marxists, and it has flowed from the peculiar vocabulary of Marxism into the peculiar vocabulary of statesmen and publicists. Distorted from its original meaning of a science of ideas, or a thinking about ideas, it has come to mean ideas themselves. It signifies a set of ideas; more particularly, and more exactly, it signifies a set of ideas relating to one particular object, or concerned with one particular sphere. That object and that sphere I can only call by the name of socio-politics. Not only does it include politics; it also includes economics (here Marxism has had its say); it even includes the whole of social life. An ideology is now a set of connected ideas, relating to the aim and method both of Society and of the State. It is doubly double-barrelled. It relates both to aim and to method—both to the purpose and to the process of community-action. It also relates both to the political and to the social aspect of the community—both to politics and to social economics. The trail of Napoleon, its first distorter, is still over the word 'ideology', but there has been a double change. In the first place, the word has become polite. It is no longer a nickname. In the second place, the word has become more largely comprehensive. It is no longer a matter of meta-politics, as it was in Napoleon's time. It is now a matter of meta-socio-politics.

There have been ideologies and conflicts of ideologies before the twentieth century. If Europe to-day seems to be divided between two ideologies (actually, as we shall see, there are more than two), so was the Europe of the sixteenth and the first half of the seventeenth centuries, during the religious wars. Two conflicting sets of ideas, Protestant and Catholic, were at grips, and sometimes, in some particular area (it might be the Netherlands, or it might be the area of the French Huguenots), there was intervention by the protagonists of one or the other set on behalf of their cause. 'Das alles', as Heine said to the lady who refused him a caress, 'Das alles...ist mir schon einmal geschehen.' Let me cite two examples of the recurrent writing which covers the palimpsest of history. We are concerned to-day with the problem of Spain, and we are asking whether it is right in the name of democracy, or in the name of Communism, or in the name of Fascism, to intervene in the affairs of Spain. In 1579, the unknown author of a famous pamphlet, the *Vindiciae contra Tyrannos*, thinking of the struggling cause of the French Huguenots, discussed in his *Quarta quaestio* 'whether neighbouring Princes rightly may, or should, give aid to the subjects of other Princes oppressed in the cause of the true religion'. That question vexed Queen Elizabeth. It is not very different from the question which vexes contemporary leaders of peoples. Another example is even more apposite. Herr Hitler proclaims the natural and inevitable enmity which exists between the Communist and the non-Communist. Oliver Cromwell, in a speech of 1656, proclaimed the natural and providential enmity between Spanish Catholics and all who stood for the true interest of God. 'Why, truly, your great enemy is the Spaniard. He is a natural enemy. He is naturally so; he is naturally so throughout, by reason of that enmity that is in him against whatsoever is of God.' Cromwell is clear that this is no mere and simple enmity of England and Spain, just as Herr Hitler is clear that his is no mere and simple enmity of Germany and Russia. 'All the honest interests', says Cromwell, 'yea, all interests of the Protestants, in Germany, Denmark, Helvetia and the Cantons, and all the interests in Christendom, are the same as yours. Be convinced what is God's interest, and prosecute it; you will find that you act for a great many who are God's own. Therefore, I say your danger is from the common enemy abroad....' It was Spain then. It is Russia now.

Analogies must not be exaggerated. They twist in our hands and defeat us. But before we leave the solid and cool ground of history for the fires that burn below the treacherous crust of the present, it may be well to mention a second period of the conflict of ideologies in the history of modern Europe. This is the period of the conflict between the ideology of Legitimism and the ideology of Liberalism in the years which followed the Congress of Vienna, a century ago. That conflict divided Europe between 1815 and 1848. Spain, no longer a protagonist as in the sixteenth century, was now a battleground. Some cried for intervention; others cried for non-intervention. There was even a time when the policy of England might be described as a policy of intervention to secure non-intervention. We can hardly say to ourselves O passi graviora, but perhaps we may say, O passi similia, and trust that God will give an end to these things too.

The war of ideas, or conflict of ideologies, in which we are told by the Communists and anti-Communists that we are plunged to-day, is a conflict of a different order from the previous wars which have just been mentioned. It does not turn on the religious basis and the religious

complexion of the community, like the religious wars of
the sixteenth century and the early seventeenth century.
More exactly, it does not turn primarily on that question;
secondarily, as we shall see, that question is still involved
in Russia, in Germany, in Italy, and indeed in Europe at
large. The past is not yet liquidated. It survives into the
present. And in any case religion, and the place of religion
in the life of the community, are not yet matters of the
past. Again, our modern war of Communist and Fascist
ideas does not, like the European struggle between 1815
and 1848, turn primarily on the political basis and the
political system of the community. The issue is not an
issue between Legitimism, in the sense of the sovereign's
right to prescriptive ownership of his acquired and vested
sovereignty, and Liberalism, in the opposite sense of the
people's right to the indefeasible enjoyment of its inherent
sovereignty. And yet that issue, too, if in an altered form
and with less of a sole or primary significance, still survives. The issue between leadership, or dictatorship, and
the claim of the community to determine its life by a free
discussion of alternatives, is still a living issue. Here again
the past is not liquidated. It survives into the present, and
it may be said of liberty, as well as of religion, that it is not
yet a matter of the past. None the less, even if the issues
of the past still survive, we are now face to face with a
war which primarily and originally seems to be of a
different order. It is different in two respects. In the first
place, it is a war which mainly turns on the social-economic
basis and the social-economic complexion of the community. It is a war between (may I put it crudely?) the
order of private enterprise and the order of communism.

In the second place, it is a war which actuates and energises, on a new scale and with a new grandeur, the whole of the population. In the old wars there were many passengers. The mass of the population, uneducated and untaught, was largely passive. To-day, with the spread of education, and the equal, or greater, spread of propaganda, we have great self-conscious populations. Mass philosophies are engaged in struggle with mass philosophies. Not only does the basis of division cut more closely to the very quick, because it touches the acute and sensitive nerve of property; it also cuts through a population which knows and feels—but more particularly feels; which hangs attentively on the struggle, and is actively engaged in its vicissitudes.

It is a simple thing to oppose the order of private enterprise and the order of communism. Indeed, it is far too simple. They are not opposites or antitheses; on the contrary, they can co-exist; and the real question of our days is the question of the proportion in which they shall co-exist in each of our States, and of the nature of that mixed economy, partly private and partly public, which each of them must necessarily build. Even in Communist Russia, as anyone will discern who reads the first chapter of the New Constitution of December 1936, there is already a mixed economy. But if it is a simple thing to oppose the order of private enterprise and the order of communism, it is a still simpler thing to oppose the cause and the party of the Fascist to the cause and party of the Communist, as if we were necessarily bound to choose the one or the other and there were no *tertium quid*, or even a *quartum quid*. No doubt, as Sir Herbert Samuel has said in a recent address to the British Institute of Philosophy, 'both the Fascist and the Communist would wish it to appear that the choice was so limited, for the support of each is recruited in large measure by hostility to the other'. We should be innocent if we allowed ourselves to be tempted into the cage of such a dilemma. We should be innocent, because we should not only be forgetting there were other alternatives, but also forgetting the fact that certainly Fascism, and probably Communism too (Communism with a large C, as a party and a cause), is far from simple. Each is complex. Each contains elements which we may like, and elements which we may dislike. Fascism, for example, is not only the cause of private enterprise; it may even be said to be disrespectful to that cause in some of its actions and implications. It is also the cause of the nation, the national organism—racially conceived in Germany as a body of pure blood, metaphysically conceived in Italy as a transcendent being—the *Volk* or *Nazione*, nerved by an internal solidarity and exultant in its external thrust. Fascism has inherited, mended and extended the mantle of nineteenth-century nationalism, however much it may boast that in its method of government it has transcended the nineteenth century and belongs to the twentieth. Not only is Fascism the cause of the nation as well as of private enterprise; it is also (at any rate when it opposes itself to Communism) the cause of religion. It supports the cause of Christian belief and the Christian Churches—at any rate in so far as they can make their peace with nationalism and nationalism can make its peace with them. One of the 'points' of the original programme of the National Socialist Party of February 1920 proclaims: 'We demand the liberty of all religious confessions in the State, so far as they do not imperil its stability or offend against the sentiment of the German race in matters of social ethics and private morality.'

Thus is constructed a triad: property, nation and religion. And this triad is then opposed to a counter-triad of common ownership, internationalism (or perhaps one should rather say *a*nationalism) and scientific materialism with its anti-God propaganda. Communism is thus depicted as hostile not only to private property and private enterprise, but also to the autonomy of the nation, however much Communist Russia may formally profess to respect in her own internal life the autonomy of what are called nationalities. Communism is identified with the Comintern, and the Comintern is shown as a crusading force resolutely refusing to stay at home within its boundaries, and resolutely determined to obliterate the dykes and boundaries of other nations—neither based on the nation within itself, nor tolerant of nations outside itself— a would-be boundless, a would-be universal society, moving, unless it be withstood, over the ruin of nations towards a single and monotonous republic of the workers of the world. This is the head and forefront of the offending of Communism, but it is not its only offence. It offends against religion as well as against the nation. It is a deluge which threatens not only the autonomy of nations, but also the liberty of religious confessions. It is a deluge against which we are summoned to take up arms by a double and even a triple call.

Such a presentation of the conflict of ideologies in terms of triad and counter-triad is obviously made from the particular angle of Fascism. The counter-triad is merely a dummy, a set of abstract negatives, erected to correspond to the supposed positives of Fascism. If we set Russian Communism to speak for itself, we shall find that it does not speak in negatives. It does not negate private property and private enterprise. On the contrary, it mixes an element of small private economy, in the shape of individual peasants and handicraftsmen, with a dominant form of public economy; it encourages piece-rates and differential wages; it even encourages Stakhanovism. Nor does it negate the nation. On the contrary, it is assuming a more and more national form, and more and more recoiling on the idea of the Russian Fatherland. Religion it does seek to negate. It is irreligious; we may even say that it is religiously irreligious. It is proclaiming, as Tom Paine did in 1794, 'the Age of Reason', but it is proclaiming it in a more drastic and anti-theistic form. None the less, there is less of negativism in the Communist creed and practice, as they stand to-day, than is allowed in the Fascist presentation. In the same way, there is less of positivism in the Fascist creed and practice than appears in its own apologies. Private property and private enterprise, as we shall have reason to notice later, are under heavy shackles in the Fascist States. Respect for the dykes and boundaries of the nations is not evident in the case of Spain, even if the movement into Spain be interpreted as merely a counter-movement to a prior Communist wave. Nor can we say that the cause of religion and the liberty of religious confession are entirely safe in Germany and in Italy. In Italy there reigns what I should call the uneasy truce established by the Conciliation Treaty, the Financial

Convention and the Concordat of February 1929. In Germany the truce is still more uneasy. Nationalism *in excelsis* is apt to say, 'Thou shalt have none other gods but me.' The German Church Minister, on the eve of the Christmas of 1936, proclaimed that the Divine order was the community ordained by God and decided by blood, the people, and that to serve it was to offer real service to God himself. Between the God who is the nation and the anti-God who is scientific materialism it is not easy to choose.

So far the argument has been confined to whittling away the edges of the antithesis or conflict of ideologies, when it is presented in the form of the conflict of Fascism and Communism. It may now proceed on another tack. We may turn to face the question, which has already reared its head, whether there are not other ideologies which must also be taken into our reckoning. There are at any rate two or three. Perhaps there are more. But two or three will suffice, and more than suffice.

In the first place there is what I should call the ideology of the Roman Catholic Church. That Church has over three hundred million adherents. They are comparable in number with the adherents of Fascism and Communism— the hundred and ten millions in Germany and Italy, and the hundred and seventy millions in Russia. The Roman Catholic Church has an ideology, in matters of social economics, which was recently set forth in the Encyclical *Quadragesimo Anno* of the year 1931. It is an ideology of private property and private enterprise, modified by old Christian doctrines of 'right use' and the *commune bonum*, and modified also by a modern conception of what may be called corporativism. The corporativism of *Quadra-gesimo Anno* has its analogies with the corporativism of Fascist Italy. It has also its fundamental differences, as any one will realise who reads the end of Part II of the Papal Encyclical, with its criticism of the system of corporations adopted in a certain anonymous State. It is not modern Italy but modern Austria which illustrates or seeks to illustrate the principles of *Quadragesimo Anno*. In any case, and whatever may be its relations to Italy or to Austria, there is here an ideology which has to be taken into account. For the moment, indeed, the policy of the Vatican, as distinct from the ideology of its Encyclicals, appears to be opposed with a fundamental opposition to Communism, and therefore allied with Fascism. There is a terror of Russian anti-theism, aided by a similar terror of Spanish anti-clericalism (a different thing from Russian anti-theism); and this terror swings the Vatican into alignment with the Fascist cause. But the alignment has its difficulties, its irregularities, its oscillations; and the day may come when the permanent ideology of the Roman Catholic Church may triumph over the temporary terrors of the Vatican.[1]

Secondly, and obviously, there is the ideology of the Liberal-Democratic States. The cardinal fact of that ideology is that it is concerned not so much with the aims as with the methods of government—not so much with its purpose as with its process. Here we have to notice that on this cardinal issue of the method and process of government, Fascism and Communism are so far from being

[1] Since this address was delivered, a new Encyclical has been issued, challenging the action of National Socialism in matters of religion.

opposed that they are similar, and even identical. The kaleidoscope has shifted: the antithesis with which we are now presented is an antithesis between the free process of discussion and the dictated uniformity of the single-party State. The Communist and the Fascist States are alike single-party States. They equally dispense with the process of discussion. It is not our English observation only which detects this congruity. It has been remarked by German theorists, and not least by that acute theorist Dr Carl Schmitt. In a pamphlet called *State, Movement and People*, he remarks that the tendency of our times is a tendency towards a new triune system, in which the dualism of the old Liberal-Democratic system (the dualism between State and Individual, or between State and Society) is transcended. In the new triune system a single movement or party is the keystone which binds, or the common inspiration which controls, the State on the one side of the arch, and the people or community or social order on the other. I quote his own words:

In the State of the German National Socialist Movement, as in the Fascist Movement of Italy, if in very different ways, this new triune system of political unity may be observed. It is generally symptomatic of the State of the twentieth century. Even in the Bolshevist State of the Soviet Union a triune system of State, Party, and Labour has been attempted as a totalitarian conception of political and social reality.

We see therefore—recognised on our own side, and recognised also on the other—another conflict of ideologies. It is the conflict between the ideology of the Liberal-Democratic States and the ideology common to the Fascist and Communist States. But here a difficulty emerges. Is it right to speak of an ideology of the Liberal-Democratic States? In one sense it is. If we accept the definition of an ideology which relates it both to aim and to method, both to the purpose and to the process of community-action, then it is just to say that the Liberal-Democratic States, by virtue of having a particular and cardinal doctrine about the method or process of government—the doctrine of discussion—have an ideology which stands opposed by its nature to the opposing doctrine professed by the Fascist and Communist States on this grave and essential issue. But in another sense it is wrong to speak of an ideology of democracy. If we look at ends or aims rather than at process or method, it is the ideology of democracy to have no ideology. It has no *single* set of connected ideas about the ends or aims of government. On the contrary, it is its essence to have a plurality of sets of ideas, represented by a plurality of parties, and to trust to the play of discussion for an accommodation and conciliation of the competing sets of ideas in some generally accepted compromise, some majority-minority agreement, on which the general life can amicably proceed.

We are thus confronted not with a simple conflict of ideologies but with a criss-cross of conflicts. On the one hand there is the conflict between Fascism and Communism, primarily relating, or supposed to relate, to ends or aims. This in itself is not a single conflict between the order of private enterprise and the order of communism: it is a mixed conflict in which religion and the nation are also invoked on the one side, and the ideas of an international community and of a purely materialistic and anti-theistic humanism are also invoked on the other. That is one conflict. On the other hand, and cutting across the conflict between Communism and Fascism, there is also the conflict which separates the States of discussion, with their plurality of parties, and with the plurality of sets of competing ideas which that implies, from the States of the single, uniform movement of thought (or should I say intuition?) with their system of a single party. Now, of these two conflicts it may be said that the second—the conflict between the States of discussion and the States of the single party—is at least as great as the first, and possibly even greater. It is not as great, or greater, in the sense that it leads as easily, or more easily, to physical warfare. It is as great, or rather I would frankly say that it is greater, in the sense that it leads to a greater tension of what Blake called the 'mental fight', in which our sword must not be allowed to sleep in our hands. The conflict engaged is the conflict between reason and anti-reason; and reason must stretch her faculties, and use her bow, her arrows, her spear, her chariot of fire. If I may venture on a paradox, I would make bold to say that in the great sphere of politics the process of life is greater than its objectives, and the method of governing superior to the aim of government. The enemies of democracy accuse it of being a legalised, or pseudo-legalised, form of standing civil war. It *is* civil war, the peaceable civil war of ideas; and in the realm of reason such civil war is peace, the tranquillity of minds engaged in the due exercise of their faculties. To keep alive the reasoning play of our individual minds (and where else does reason reside?) is the great thing to which we are called. It may be that we are all icebergs, with only one-ninth of ourselves emerging above the waters of instinct into the light of reason. But it is the ninth part that matters. The great thing is that we should govern ourselves in the light, and 'fairly put our minds to one another'. The single movement, the single party, retreats into the depths of the unconscious. It weds the unconscious instinct of the led to the unconscious and somnambulistic intuition of the leader. It conjures up masses and magnitudes—proletariat, or race, or transcendent national organism—unknown to sober thought, but accepted none the less as the objects of an absorbed and absorbing loyalty, and tending to conflict, as icebergs conflict, in the dark. The great self-conscious population which becomes conscious of something which is not itself, but which it is taught and led to identify with itself, is a new phenomenon. It is, or it may be, a volcano as well as an iceberg. All the more reason why we should be ready to pit, not in physical warfare, but in mental fight, the ideology based on the value of individual thought and mutual discussion against the ideology based on the value of group-emotion and collective magnetisation.

In any case this new phenomenon of our times is a phenomenon common to Communist and Fascist States. In regard to the process of politics, and on the ground of method of government, they do not greatly differ from one another, if indeed they differ at all; but they differ greatly from States in which the method and process of the free discussion of alternative aims and policies is still in operation. It may be added that Fascist and Communist States do not differ from one another as greatly as they appear to differ, or allege that they differ, even on the ground of social economics. The contrast between the order of private enterprise and the order of communism, as has been said already, is far from absolute. The contrast between the economic policy of a Fascist State and that of a Communist State is still less absolute. If Russia mixes a small private economy with a dominant form of public economy, it may also be said that Germany and Italy—and perhaps particularly Italy—mix a considerable element of public economy with a not very dominant form of private economy. They nationalise much of production and exchange on the basis of an ideal of autarcy, or self-sufficiency, which has its military as well as its economic motive. They introduce what may be called, by an adaptation of Fichte's phrase, *Der geschlossene Autarkiestaat*. This is not so very different from Russian Communism, except that Russian Communism seeks to communalise production, distribution and exchange not so much on the basis of an ideal of self-sufficiency, though that is also there, as on the basis of an ideal of the even and wide diffusion of peaceful human happiness. When Signor Mussolini, in his speech of 23 March 1936, foreshadowed 'the nationalisation of all basic industries of importance for the purpose of national defence', he was proclaiming a policy at once like and unlike that of Communism. When the German Government, as it does, 'regulates the whole of external trade', 'exercises a decisive influence on the course of investment and the development of industrial enterprise', and 'extends the control of prices to all products',[1] it may be outside the order of communism, but it is not inside the order of private enterprise.

There is still a third factor, and that not the least, which

[1] The phrases are quoted from the last report of the Director of the International Labour Office, Twentieth Session, 1936, p. 51.

cuts across the facile theory of the single and engulfing conflict between the ideology of Fascism and the ideology of Communism. More exactly, there is another war of ideas or battle of doctrines which may more easily outrun the area of mental fight, and run into actual and physical war, than any other. This is the conflict between the static ideology of the contented States, and the dynamic ideology of the States which are hungry and discontented. Whether the hunger of the discontented State be interpreted as a demographic fact, due to the pressure of population and the absence of an adequate supply of raw materials, or whether it be interpreted as a fact of the spiritual order, due to an urgent desire for prestige and a status in the hierarchy of the world more commensurate with a deep sense of race or nationality—whichever it be (and there is much to be said for the second interpretation), the hunger is there, and it breeds its own ideology. In Fascism and in National Socialism one of the deepest elements is the idea of growth, change, becoming, expansion, and the ultimate *Reich* or *Impero*. We who repose upon an acquired empire, and who have about us, even if that empire should pass and dissolve, the shadow of a mighty name for a mantle, must reckon with these elements. They spell something more than militarism. They spell the idea of change as the strongest son of life; and if they also spell war, or preparation for war, they spell these things as the servants of change. Here is a great question of our days—a riddle of the Sphinx of history who watches the process and the changes of time. How can change come, if it be not by the midwifery of war? It is no answer to that riddle, at any rate for those who believe in change, to plead the cause of collective security. That cause is no ideal for those who challenge the very idea of security, with its beatitude for the possessor; who acclaim the venture, and are ready t) fly into the unknown. They have to be met, if they can be met, by a frank discussion of change. If change can come by discussion, that will be the greatest triumph of discussion. And at any rate discussion is a better midwife than war.

But these are large issues. In the immediate present the conflict between the ideology of the static and the ideology of the dynamic States introduces a new complication. The kaleidoscope changes. Communist Russia now seeks to take her place by the side of the Liberal-Democratic States in defending the cause of a static ideology in international affairs. Perhaps the new company which she is seeking to keep has been the great factor which has tended of late to draw Russia, even in the sphere of her own internal life, towards a formal approximation to the general democratic system of ideas. The vortex of the major conflict, between the dynamic ideology and the static, has tossed a heaving ship away from the system of a single movement and party (still present in fact, but at any rate modified in form) towards a system of the Rights of Man, expounded in the tenth chapter of the New Constitution, of universal suffrage and territorial constituencies, of general parliamentarianism. The more Russia changes, many will say, the more she remains the same. That may be, or it may not be. In form, at any rate, there is change. In another quarter too there is change in Russia. The old Russia, in the days of Dostoievsky, once poured her national fervour into the mould of the orthodox Church. The new Russia, which in 1917 turned away from nationalism, is now beginning again to pour national fervour into a new Holy Russia, the consecrated soil of a national system of Communism. Russia is recoiling upon herself; drawing back upon the dykes and boundaries of her own national life; ready, it would even appear, to respect the dykes and boundaries of other nations. It is an attitude natural to a nation (provided it feels itself to be a nation) which possesses one-sixth of the habitable globe, and may well feel content with its portion.

What is to be said in conclusion? There is, as I see the matter, no clean and simple dilemma. The picture I see is the picture Alcæus saw—the gusts of veering gales; the waves rolling hither and thither; the dark ship borne in their midst. To be a pure friend of Communism is to forget that it tends to make man a bit of plastic clay instead of a living source of individual initiative and individual responsibility—clay, too, unleavened by any particle of the Divine breath. But to be a pure enemy of Communism is to forget that, if it abnegates private enterprise (and even that it does not do wholly), and if again it eschews religion, it is also moving towards the idea of a sovereign internal Constitution, and towards the parallel idea, in the international sphere, of a stable and permanent system of Europe. To be a pure friend of Fascism is to forget that it tends to substitute a generated mass-enthusiasm for the reasoning and reasonable process of discussion; that it tends to exalt the dynamic movement of the nation into explosive dynamite; that it tends, for all its devotion to the order of private enterprise and the cause of religion, to make a regimented system of autarcy prior to private enterprise, and the idea of the nation prior to the idea of the religious society. But to be a pure enemy of Fascism is to forget that democratic forms of discussion may be degraded into a collusive game for lucrative stakes, which had better be ended; the national unity, where it has not been fully achieved, is a precious thing, for which men may well be passionate; that change and growth, if they be not all, are at any rate part of the life of nations, and will find out the way for themselves if a way is not found out for them.

Are there, then, any fixed points? First, we may take it for granted, if the argument has any value, that there is no sweeping dilemma in Europe. There is rather, if we look at things in their totality, and not through coloured spectacles, with one glass Russian red, and the other Italian black, or German brown—there is rather a trilemma or a pentalemma. The reflection is comforting. There is more safety in a number of criss-crossing antitheses than in a single antithesis. Secondly, situated as we are, and standing in the faith of Liberal democracy, we, for our part, have to be true to our faith, both nationally and internationally. Nationally, we have to argue, if they will let us, with our own Fascists and Communists (and not least with the latter, for perhaps with wealth distributed among us as unequally as it is we need them most): we have to learn from them, if they will teach us, whatever of Truth is in them. Internationally, we have to say that we stand for the right of Spain to argue out her own affairs, even at the point of the sword; and we have equally, and even more, to say that we are ready ourselves to argue out, not at the point of the sword, but with the good edge of reason, the problems of change and readjustment which vex, and not unjustly vex, the dynamic and electric States. The temper that closes down discussion at home, and prefers abroad the *acta* of sudden hammer-strokes to the agenda of the conference and the council room, must be met by the temper which courts and invites discussion both at home and abroad.

Finally, we need not despair of all this ἀνέμων στάσις— all these conflicting gusts of the veering gale of doctrine. Sophocles speaks somewhere of the blast of direful winds that *hushes* the groaning ocean. It may be so to-day. Perhaps these direful winds are a way of peace rather than of war. Perhaps they are a vent, or substitute, for that which might be war. When men argue hotly, fisticuffs are not always at hand. Europe is a great stadium of argument to-day. Let the causes say their say. They have to express themselves; and it is better to listen in the crowded ring in which we all sit than to interrupt and brawl. Our continent is a richer thing in the treasures of the mind than it was thirty years ago. It is not altogether evil that great gusts of doctrine should sweep over it and vex it. It may even be counted for good that Europe should be so much one that it can be vexed, like a single sea, by all these embattled winds of conflicting ideologies.

II
THE BREAKDOWN OF
DEMOCRACY

Delivered before the Liberal Summer School at Cambridge, 4 August 1933

'The Breakdown of Democracy.' I deny my title. To affirm such a thing is to make the admission that the free spirit of man has broken down and ceased to be free. We do not say that the law of gravitation, the great law of the action of material bodies in space, has broken down because Einstein has arisen. Neither should we say that the principle of democracy, the great principle of the action of the human spirit in the organised societies which it has constructed, has broken down because on the Left and the Right—in Russian Communism and in Italian and German Fascism—the grandiose figure of the would-be dictator of the human spirit has emerged. Not that there is any real parallel between Einstein and Hitler. The one has modified our conception of natural law by a new discovery. The other is seeking to change our conception of human principle by taking us back to the ancient blood-group, or clan, in which the only spirit is that of the Group, and its only expression is the mind and will of the Leader. But it is one thing to go with Einstein on a new sort of voyage through space. It is another thing to go with Hitler on a voyage back through time into the ancient Hercynian forest.

Before we speak of breakdown, we must first of all look at the facts—the facts of geography, and then (for a moment's space) the facts of history. Geographically, and confining ourselves in the first instance to Europe, we can see a great area to the West of the Rhine (for many years past a river of division in European thought) where democracy is not dead. In that area are the democracies of England, France and Spain; of the Scandinavian countries; of Belgium and Holland. So far as that goes, and so far as Europe to-day is concerned, it would seem that democracy is mainly a Western phenomenon. But there are two other things to be said. In the first place, the division of Europe at the boundary of the Rhine is not a new thing. Ever since the Romantic movement began in Germany, about 1770, there has tended to be a division between thought and politics to the West of the Rhine, and thought and politics to the East. To the East of the Rhine there has lived a Romantic philosophy of the *Volk*, or personified people, as a super-spirit or super-person somehow transcending the individual spirit and person of each of its members—singing its own *Volkslieder* in its own *Volkssprache*; creating its own *Volksrecht*; constructing its own *Volksstaat*; in a word, engulfing 'organically' in the sweep of its own perpetual becoming the life of all its members. This is a philosophy which culminated in Hegel and in Hegel's disciple Marx, who simply transferred to the idea of class the attributes which Romanticism had previously vindicated for the idea of the Folk. It is a philosophy which has spread—here in a Marxian and there in a Hegelian form—to Russia and Italy. It is a philosophy which, furnished with the new jet of the idea of Aryan race-purity, has been fanned into an ardent flame in Germany to-day. There is nothing new in the contrast between anti-democratic Romanticism, with its cult of the group, and democratic liberalism, with its belief in the intrinsic value of the individual; and if in Europe to-day democratic liberalism is mainly confined to the West, we can comfort ourselves by reflecting that it has not lost ground which it had ever permanently won. But there is also another comfort, and another thing to be said. If we look outside Europe, we can hardly say that democracy is a losing cause. It still informs the British Commonwealth. It still informs most of the continent of America. And if we look at the continent of Asia, shall we say that democracy is dead or dying when in India and China, which contain nearly half of the human race, democratic ideas imported from the West (as the wind carries seeds on its wings) are struggling for growth and development?

So far of geography. One brief word may be added by way of historical retrospect. Twenty years ago, in 1913, there were three great Empires in Europe—Germany, Russia and Austria-Hungary—and an Emperor was the central figure and (as a German thinker would say) 'the bearer of the authority of the State' in each of the three. To-day, in 1933, these Empires are all gone. It is hard to say what permanent organisation will take the place of the German Empire of twenty years ago. But it may safely be said that there is already more of democracy to-day in the old dominions of the Hapsburgs—in Prague, in Vienna, in Cracow—than there was in 1913. It may also be said, not without fear of contradiction, but yet with some measure of confidence, that there is more of the spirit of democracy to-day in Leningrad and Moscow than there was in 1913. We have to say to ourselves, 'Perspective', and yet again, 'Perspective'. We live in turbulent and moving times. More particularly, at this moment, we live among economic exigencies, which affect the normal play of political institutions. It is hard to discern the set of the tide. We can only fix our eye on great landmarks, and endeavour to judge our course quietly by the guidance which they give. So far as I see, the great landmarks give us no reason for despair.

But what, after all, is democracy? For our purposes, and from the point of view of our argument, we may say that it is two things. It is a principle of the action of the human spirit—the principle that free spirits, in the area of social and political as well as of individual life, should freely guide themselves to freely determined issues. It is also a system of institutions, operative in a political community, which enables this principle to be realised and serves as the means of its realisation.

In this statement both these things are essentially interconnected; and both of them must be present in order to constitute democracy in the full and general sense of the word. This connection has been denied. In the literature of Italian Fascism, and more particularly in Mussolini's essay on *La Dottrina del Fascismo*, an antithesis is drawn between what we have called the principle of action, and what we have termed the system of institutions. The one is defined as the creed of Liberalism, and the other as the essence of Democracy—and Liberalism and Democracy, thus defined and distinguished, are treated not as allies or complements, but as mutually exclusive enemies. Liberalism, upon this view, is *laissez-faire*: it is a warning to the State to leave the individual to his own devices: it is

J. S. Mill; it is Manchester. Democracy, as contrasted with liberalism, is the right of a whole people to control itself, and thereby all its members, by the force of arithmetic and the method of majority-vote: it is a warning to the individual will to submit to the will of the number; it is Rousseau; it is Geneva.

Now we may distinguish liberalism and democracy in thought, but we cannot oppose them as opposites. Liberalism and democracy are two sides of a single coin. The essential stuff of which the coin is made is individual human personality. This is the intrinsic value which must serve as our standard of measurement. Because individual human personality has an intrinsic value, and because its development is the ultimate end, two consequences follow which are linked to one another by a natural sympathy. The first is that each individual should be guaranteed and secured the conditions under which he can develop freely. Those conditions were once designated, in an old English phrase, by the name of civil and religious liberty. But civil and religious liberty is not enough. There is also an area of economic liberty—including in its broad scope the various conditions necessary for the free development of all the millions of workers in industry—which it is the peculiar problem of our age to discover and define and secure. This brings us to the second consequence. The only way of discovering the general sum of conditions which is necessary to the free development of individuals is the way of free debate and discussion among individuals. The second consequence, therefore, of the basis from which we start is that each individual should be free to express his views on the general affairs of his community; free to join in the great and healthy process of discussion which, acting through its various organs, determines the conditions under which we all live and the rights we all enjoy; free, in a word, to participate in that energy of democratic self-government which is also, as J. S. Mill argued, a great and ennobling way of individual self-development.

We may call these two consequences, if we will, by two different names. We may say that the one is the cause of liberalism proper, and the other the cause of democracy, in the more specific sense of the word. But they are really twin consequences, issuing equally from the same basis; and there is no quarrel between them. Liberalism, if it is genuinely derived from its own true basis, is also democratic; and in the same way, and in the same condition, democracy is also liberal. Democracy, even if we confine the term to its more specific sense, is something more than the mass weight of number, and something greater than a mode of government by mathematics. It is a way of giving to each individual person, as such and because he is such, a voice and an influence in determining the conditions of life in his community. Democracy is not, in its essence (though it is in one of its external forms), a matter of voting. It is not a method of government by counting heads instead of breaking them. It is a method of government by laying heads together, in a common debate in which all share, to attain a result which as many as possible are agreed in accepting. Dr Johnson once said of a man he admired, 'He is a fine fellow, sir; he fairly puts his mind to yours.' This saying touches the true significance of democracy. It means, where it succeeds, that we all attain a higher measure of human dignity, because all of us 'fairly put our minds' to the minds of others. It means government by discussion; and that is its inward essence. Apart from any system of institutions which it involves, it demands a gift for participation in a rational process of common deliberation.

To join in a rational process of common deliberation is not an easy thing. It requires a large measure of self-control. Discussion is not a battle, waged with personal passion for the sake of personal victory. It is a co-operative enterprise, conducted for the sake of attaining the greatest possible measure of general agreement. But it is not easy to lay heads together without rubs. It is hard to put one's mind fairly to the mind of another man without a jar. Discussion between different views and different political parties is a necessary part of democracy; but if views become opinionated and parties intransigent, discussion may readily pass into collision, and co-operative enterprise may degenerate into sheer war. Nor is this all. It is hard to keep the spirit keyed to the pitch of rational discussion. Emotion is always waiting for its opportunity. A community which is not on the watch may easily slip down with a run into the abandonment of mere group-sentiment. It may do so all the more easily because the art of advertisement and mass-suggestion, nowadays so highly developed, can readily play entrancing tunes to stir the emotions. When this is done, and done successfully, the high democratic art of rational discussion is abnegated. An induced unanimity of emotion takes its place. The basis of emotion may be class, as it is in Russia. It may be race, as it is in Germany. It may be nation—the nation as a higher personality, superior to all its members, the very *anima dell' anima*—as it is in Italy. Whatever it be, it is the opposite of that basis of individual human personality on which democracy rests, and from which democracy results. Whatever it be, it necessarily entails, at any rate for the time being, a breakdown of democracy.

Will such a breakdown last? Must we contemplate the disappearance of democracy, at any rate from a great part of Europe, as an historic and outworn form? Our answer to such questions must depend in the last resort on our view of the spirit of man. We may say, with Shakespeare, 'What a piece of work is a man! How noble in reason, how infinite in faculties!' Or we may say, as some are now beginning to say, 'Men in the mass are a managed multitude, and those who have the art of management had better practise it, and indeed have the right to practise it, whether as dictator for the proletariat, or as Führer for the coming Aryan race, or as Duce of the higher personality of the nation.' The choice is before us; and the responsibility is with the chooser. Those who choose the first alternative may take this comfort to themselves, that they believe in the reasonable and self-determining mind of man, and that sooner or later, in the process of his long education, man will justify their belief.

We have spoken of the democratic process of discussion as acting through various organs, and thus involving a system of institutions. We may say that this system of institutions includes four essential organs of discussion, through which the general community and all its members are able to determine freely the conditions of their common life. The four organs are party, electorate, parliament and cabinet. They are arranged like a pyramid, in an ascending series, with discussion initiated at the first stage, but assuming a more intense and responsible quality at each later stage, because it approaches nearer the point of final decision. But the analogy of the pyramid is pictorial rather than real. We must not press it to the point of arguing either that party and party-formation should dominate the whole because they are the basis, or that cabinet and cabinet-guidance shall dominate everything because they are the apex. The proper working of a democratic system of institutions depends on a curious and delicate balance, in which each of the four factors keeps its place, and while making its specific contribution to the process of government by discussion claims nothing more than the right to make that specific contribution. We may illustrate this general idea of balance by reference to the particular place and the specific contribution of parliament. Parliament has to carry discussion, begun already in the electorate, and, even before that, in the parties which place their views and their candidates before the electorate, to a higher stage in which it begins to impinge upon and to affect the decision of the cabinet. In carrying discussion to this higher stage, and thus making its own specific contribution, parliament must balance itself in its place between the electorate on the one side and the cabinet on the other. It has to do two different things in regard to either, and to do them both simultaneously. As regards the electorate, it has both to pay due regard to previous discussion and voting upon issues among the electors, and to discuss these issues anew itself with a sense of its own responsibility. As regards the cabinet, it has both to exert an influence on the policy of the cabinet by the force of its own discussion, and to leave the cabinet free to form its policy freshly by its own deliberation on its own responsibility. The illustration will show the delicacy of the balance of a democratic system of institutions. The delicacy of that balance will serve to explain the difficulty of working such a system. That difficulty will in turn explain why we may well have minor breakdowns, at this or that point of the system, from time to time. But it may also suggest that we need not despair if such breakdowns occur. The balance has been disturbed. It is our business to get to work, and to seek to restore the balance. One organ has got out of gear, and is running, as it were, free. We must seek to engage it again, and to make it play its proper part in the system.

The particular problem of democracy at the present time is party. It is not the only difficulty. The electorate will create difficulties if it seeks to go beyond its specific contribution of general discussion and the election of members to carry discussion further, and if it seeks to be a co-partner with parliament and cabinet by way of referendum and initiative. Parliament will create difficulties, if it, too, seeks to go beyond its specific contribution—the general discussion of the lines of cabinet policy—and if it attempts to control the cabinet by a system of committees which drastically interferes with its responsibility. The cabinet will create difficulties, and may even put the whole system out of gear, if it grows impatient of debate, and if if throws itself into the arms of a congenial party at the expense of both parliament and electorate. But the particular difficulty of our times is party; and it is most of all a difficulty when it leaps to victory over parliament and electorate, and governs 'totalitarianally' through a party leader who dominates his colleagues and turns even the cabinet itself from an organ of discussion into a mouthpiece of decision.

Party, in its own true nature, is both an organ of discussion in itself, at the first or primary stage of that process, and a constituent element in a general scheme of organised discussion, in which it duly co-operates with other elements. Because it is an organ of discussion in itself, at the first or primary stage, we must necessarily assume the existence of a plurality of parties. It takes at least two parties to create the beginnings of public discussion; and it may be a healthy thing, for the sake of proper discussion of all the great alternatives by which a community may be confronted, that there should be more than two. Secondly, because party formations are one of the constituent elements in the general scheme of organised discussion, they must recognise the existence and the functions of other elements. They must seek to aid and support, but not to control or dominate, the operation of those elements: they must adjust themselves to the whole, and not claim that the whole shall be adjusted to them. When democracy begins to break down, or to run slowly and heavily, it is generally because party passion refuses to allow one or other of these consequences to be drawn. If we look at the matter historically, and consider events as they happen in order of time, we shall generally find that it is the second consequence which is first denied and rejected. Parties refuse to recognise the independent existence and the separate functions of the other organs of discussion. They seek to control and dominate the electorate by a system of 'integral' proportional representation under which it is only allowed to vote for prepared party lists, with the candidates already arranged in the order in which they are to be chosen. Going further, they challenge the independence of parliament, as an organ of free discussion; and the various party caucuses settle in advance the lines to be taken and the votes to be given with a sole regard to party interest and party discipline. When these things happen, the working of a democratic system of institutions has already been gravely impeded; and meanwhile party passions have also been exacerbated, partly by the process of cutting and paring the electorate as if it were a cheese, and partly by the warfare of the different caucuses in parliament. In the exacerbation of party feeling the next step may then be taken. The first and the most elementary consequence which follows from the very nature of party may be rejected. The principle that there must necessarily be a plurality of parties begins to be scouted. One party resolves, instead of discussing issues and policies with the rest, to eliminate them all, and to rule alone. This is what has happened in Italy and Germany. A single party, claiming to be the sole depositary of an alleged idea of national personality or racial purity, has established a monopoly of power. It has eliminated all other parties: and not content with dominating electorate and parliament, it has reduced them both to ghosts, pleading that the living 'leader' is the true and authentic voice of the whole community. Party, formed for discussion, has killed the discussion for which it was formed. One of the means has destroyed the end. Democracy has perished at the hands of one of its children.

There is a sentence in *La Dottrina del Fascismo* which admirably expresses the new régime. 'A party which governs a nation totalitarianally is a new fact in history.' It is indeed a new fact; and it is also a sad fact. It means two new and sad things. It means the government of one party, which has no need to debate with other parties, for the simple reason that there are none, or to adjust itself to other organs, because it has already assimilated other organs to itself. It means again that this government, thus immune from the salt of criticism, is also exempt from any limits to the area of its operation. Free to play on the minds of all by a monopoly of the means of publicity, it is also free to play on every sphere of life. That is the sense of the word totalitarian. No sphere of voluntary activity and no voluntary institution—neither economics, nor religion, nor education: neither trade union, nor church, nor university—can escape the logic of that word. It was the tendency of parties in some European countries, even when parties were multiple, to seek to engulf the lives of their members, and to provide them with party trade unions, party sports clubs, party methods of education, and a general party apparatus of life. That tendency attains its apotheosis when a single party swallows the rest, and arms itself with the whole power of the State to provide a total inspiration, which is also a total control, for every citizen. The new absolutism which is thus installed is far more drastic than any of the old absolutist monarchies. A party, knit together by party enthusiasm and united by a common devotion to its leader, is a far more efficient agent than a monarch and his advisers. The cause of liberty is meeting to-day one of the greatest foes which it has ever encountered.

If we ask ourselves why party has thus been accentuated, until it has become an end in itself, we shall readily find a number of causes. Some of them may be called universal, because they are operative everywhere. There is the universal fact of the professional politician—the paid organiser who lives by his party and naturally exalts the organisation by which he lives. Deeper than that, there is the universal fact that parties are everywhere drawn into the grave social and economic issues of our times, and are led to regard their solutions as the only possible solutions of these stirring and rending issues. In a moving world, in which new social strata are seeking to thrust themselves upward (here an impoverished middle class, and there a depressed proletariat), parties become the instruments and organs of social change. They cease to be based on merely political principles, if indeed they ever were: they seek to become philosophers of life, and to mould all life into the image of their philosophy. But besides these general causes, which are common to the civilised world, we may also trace particular causes which belong to particular countries. In Germany, for example, the nation is not even agreed about the ultimate foundations of its life and the whole basis of its future. It is confronted—if we may borrow the title of a book written by a sympathetic student of its life, M. Vienot —by *les incertitudes allemandes*. Shall it become a Communist society? Shall it take the form of a system of State-regulated Socialism? Shall it permanently assume the shape of a nationalist Aryan Folk devoted to the doctrine of blood and purity of race? When a nation is face to face with uncertainties so profound, its parties will inevitably be passionate and wage a passionate war of extermination.

The past history and tradition of German parties, as well as their present problems, serve to explain their absolute temper. Observers have long remarked their doctrinaire spirit, which makes them uncompromising and intractable. They cultivate an exclusive ideology, and they cherish a passion for realising that ideology to the nth degree. This spirit and this passion are by no means entirely the fault of the parties themselves, or of the nation behind the parties. They are largely an inheritance from the old pre-War absolutist system, which deprived parties of any real chance of responsibility, and of the chastening and moderating effects of responsibility. Parties were not built into a system of democratic institutions, as one of the essential organs of that system. They stood on the circumference of an alien system; and isolated as they were, they were driven to isolate themselves still further. It takes time to shed the inheritance of the past; and Germany is still labouring to-day under that inheritance.

Whatever the causes, particular or general, we are confronted to-day by the problem of party. Party is necessary for democracy; but we have to make party safe for democracy. This was the issue which vexed the sage and much-travelled Ulysses of English politics, Lord Bryce. His hope came to be fixed in an expert and impartial second chamber, which would be a sort of Solon in the strife of parties, and would stand, as Solon said of himself, 'throwing a strong shield over all, and not allowing any to carry the day unfairly'. It is not easy to dress ourselves in that hope. No single institution, and least of all a reformed second chamber, can be our salvation. What hopes are we then to cherish, and what way of salvation shall we advocate?

First of all, we may say that a system of government by discussion demands a certain temper of mind, which it is our bounden duty to cultivate, both individually and as a nation. It demands a common acceptance of the rules of national discussion and the standing orders of national debate—unwritten rules and orders which require abstinence from imputation and innuendo, jibes and personalities, flouts and jeers, unless such flouts and jeers be administered in that happy spirit of chaff and teasing which only a master of tact can ever possess. Again, it involves a gallant readiness to accept defeat, when the electorate has pronounced its verdict. No party (and least of all a traditional party rooted in social connections) is justified in using social power or social influence to defeat or avert the verdict of national debate. Again, and above all, a system of government by discussion demands a quality of mind which we may call by the name of agreement to differ. In other words, it demands agreement on the general lines of the national constitution and the general trend of national development, coupled with genuine difference on particular policies and programmes. It is here, and at this point, that a radical difficulty emerges. There are those who believe that redistribution of wealth and equalisation of status (which, it may safely be prophesied, the future has in store for us in any case) must be achieved immediately by a sudden break. *Their* policies and programmes, they argue, necessarily involve a rejection of some of the lines of the constitution, and a departure from much of the trend of national development. Such an argument is in itself a challenge to the temper of democracy; and the policy in which it issues is a challenge to democratic institutions. The policy is a policy of dictatorship (though it may be called by the softer name of emergency power), issuing from a single chamber, responsible only to the party majority in that chamber, and uncriticised and unchecked by the courts of law which, for centuries past, have acted as the guardians of the constitution. The danger of such a policy is less its own realisation than the realisation of its opposite. Few of us would seriously fear an effective dictatorship of the Left. Many of us might seriously fear the rapid emergence of a real dictatorship of the Right, by way of instant reaction against any appearance of dictatorship on the Left. The only dictatorial power that could actually be established in Great Britain is that of the great professional class which is so strongly entrenched, by its very functions of direction and management, in our national life. May it never be inspired to make the attempt; and may the quiet process of victory by general conviction never be displaced by the *élan* of victory through a *coup d'état*.

Democracy not only requires an appropriate temper: it also requires appropriate institutions. Not the least important of those institutions, especially in its bearing on party, is the electorate, and the methods by which the electorate votes. Here, so far as the evidence goes, it would appear to suggest that a method of voting by the method of proportional representation ultimately tends, when it is pushed to its logical conclusions, to accentuate and exacerbate party, and to make it assume the character of an end in itself, and not a means in a system of democratic government. If each party can be assured of its proportionate share, every party will do its utmost to

secure that share. There is indeed a great difference between the system which is advocated for England by the
Proportional Representation Society and the integral
systems of some other countries which only allow the
voter to vote for prepared party lists in many-member
constituencies. But if we once begin to listen to the logic
of mathematics, we may easily be driven by that logic
beyond our original intention. If we desire to escape the
growth of over-mighty parties, and if we prefer to keep
a member in close touch with his constituency rather than
assign him directly to his party, we shall be wise to keep
the single-member constituency and a simple method of
voting. By the logic of mathematics they may be dubious.
But the real question we have to solve is not a question of
mathematical logic. It is a question of what best suits the
logic—and not only the logic, but also the life—of democracy. Dictators have sometimes climbed to power on
the ruined steps of proportional representation.

We have not only to consider the old institutions and
methods of democracy. We have also to consider the
possibility of new methods and institutions: we have to
ask ourselves whether their adoption may not help to
preserve a balance, and to prevent party, or any other
existing organ, from becoming unduly dominant. Some
have advocated a National Council of Industry, or an
economic sub-parliament, which might provide another
forum than that of parliament and its parties for the
discussion of economic issues. It is not clear that these
grave issues can ever be considered fruitfully by any body
other than parliament; nor is it likely that the divisions in
an economic sub-parliament would be less acute than

those in parliament itself. But there are other methods and organs of discussion which are already beginning to be tried, and which are well worthy of our attention. In particular, there is the method of consultation, in many of the ministries in Whitehall, between official experience inside and the free expert outside. Some of us have joined, for example, in the constant discussions which are always on foot at the Board of Education, and we have seen those discussions issue in educational policies of the very first order of importance, such as the policy of the Hadow Report. This is a new development of the democratic principle of discussion: and here democracy is using its essential principle to enlist in its service the expert advice and the general experience to be found in the civic community. It is a matter of happy augury that the executive side of government should thus be devising new methods of discussion which bring the expert and the spirit of science into the service of democracy. There has been some criticism, in recent years, of the new despotism of bureaucracy. Should there not also be some praise of the new democracy of the bureaucrats?

There is one last way of making party safe for democracy which lies open before us all. If we wish for the continuance of democracy—and it may safely be said that every man in Great Britain does—it is our bounden duty to see to it that our party seeks to work out the fundamental principle of the intrinsic value of human personality in its application to the economic life of our nation. The days are gone in which we can be content with the eighteenth-century ideal of civil and religious liberty, or the nineteenth-century ideal of political liberty and a free vote for every citizen. To-day it is laid upon the Liberal party—and indeed upon all parties—to have some vision of the new economic liberty which has still to be won, and which will make every worker a free man co-operating freely in a free system of industry. There are different ways of attaining that liberty, and every party may advocate its own way. But every party has to think out, and to advocate, *some* way. It would be a grave exacerbation of party, and a serious menace to democracy, if one party stood alone in calling men to a new Jerusalem, and the rest were still content to offer the ancient shibboleths of the old. Those who belong to the Liberal party may well congratulate, as true servants of democracy, the members who joined in producing, in 1928, the vision which they called by the name of Britain's Industrial Future. So long as an old and historic party can think in such terms, and bring such a contribution into the forum of discussion, there is no great reason to fear the breakdown of democracy in our country. But the duty of our own party is also the duty of all other parties. Within the lines of our national constitution, and within the general trend of our national development, all parties are essentially bound, by their very nature as organs of democracy, to think and to ponder how the fundamental principle of democracy can be introduced more fully into the field of economic life and organisation. The greatest way of making democracy safe to-day is that all our parties should join in discussing how best it can be carried further. It will only break down if it is made to stand still.

III

THE PROSPECTS FOR
DEMOCRACY

Delivered at Chatham House, 15 March 1934

'Our epoch is not particularly gay; but it is passion-
ately interesting. It is not a heap of ruins; it is a
building-yard in which, to the sound of saws and
trowels and hammers, a world is being erected.'

The words are those of M. Joseph Barthélemy, in a
work of the year 1931 on the crisis of contemporary
democracy.[1] They are encouraging; and they are true.
No old Liberal—a species of which I am an undesponding
specimen—need beat his breast to-day. Much of London
has been pulled down. It has all been rebuilt, or is now
in the building. Much of the world has gone into liquida-
tion. It will emerge from the receiver's hands. A great
and convulsive war was fought from 1914 to 1918. Such a
war does not end in peace: at any rate it does not end in
the peace which is tranquillity. If we said to ourselves, in
1919,

> Fair Quiet, have I found thee here,
> And Innocence thy sister dear?

the answer we received was a blunt 'No'. But if we did
not find quiet and innocence, we found a building-yard.
At first it seemed as if the building was to proceed with an
American rapidity of construction. In 1920 we might
hope that the war to end war had ended in a League of

[1] *La Crise de la démocratie contemporaine*, 1931. Paris: Sirey.

Nations, and the war to make the world safe for democracy had issued in a rich harvest of new democratic constitutions. Three Empires, all more or less autocratic, had perished: there were Republics in Berlin and Vienna, in Prague and Warsaw, in Kovno and Helsingfors. But a change seemed to come in 1922. The building was not yet done; and a new type of construction began to appear. If autocracies had yielded place to republics, democracies now began to disappear before dictatorships. By 1930 there was a serried series of these dictatorships. They were of different forms. One, in Belgrade, was monarchical, and another, in Angora, presidential. Others, in Madrid and Warsaw, were military. A third form—exemplified, if exemplified very differently, alike in Rome and in Moscow, and exemplified in Moscow even before 1922—was the dictatorship of a party. Differing in the forms which they assumed, these dictatorships also differed in the ends which they sought to achieve. Some were dictatorships of the Right; others were dictatorships of the Left; and one—the dictatorship of Mustapha Kemal, with its mixture of sweeping reform and authoritarian control—might be said to include both the Left and the Right. Since 1930 dictatorship has vanished from Madrid; but it has entered in Berlin and Vienna. Some would even say that it has entered in Washington. But the President of the United States, by the terms of its constitution, is always a potential dictator; and when he is backed by Congress, or the country, or both, the potentiality becomes actuality, legal actuality. *Vixere fortes ante* Franklin Roosevelt. Abraham Lincoln and Woodrow Wilson were also dictators in their heyday.

We seem to be confronted by a great and universal trend which sets against democracy. But we must not be too hasty. We have still to analyse the nature of dictatorship. We have still to analyse the nature of its relation to democracy, which may not, in the last resort, be a relation of pure antithesis or antagonism. But even before we attempt this analysis, there is one thing which, for the sake of balance and perspective, ought to be said at once. Whatever may be our opinion of democratic institutions, it would be absurd to maintain that the democratic spirit —the spirit of interest in general community problems, the spirit of general participation in their solution—has really receded in the last dozen years. On the contrary, there has never been a time in human history when, in all countries, the minds of men were more arrested by political problems, or more intent on debating and (if it be possible) solving these problems, than they are to-day. If the world is a building-yard, it is crowded with busy workers and thinkers. Many as are the 'anvils and hammers working', they are not more 'than there be pens and heads there sitting by their studious lamps, musing, searching, revolving new notions and ideas wherewith to present, as with their homage and fealty, the approaching reformation'. If, in a preliminary way, we may assume that democracy is a temper and a habit of free discussion of ideas—of free competition between ideas —when shall we say that there was more of that temper and habit than in these days? Why are we here to-night? Did we feel the burden of our responsibility so much thirty years ago? But it is not mainly of us in England that I am thinking. I am thinking of the immemorial

East, awaking from the sleep of custom and the ancient yoke of authority; I am thinking of India and China, and the political ideas which are surging even in Asia itself. And may it not also be said that if there are closed areas in Europe—areas of a single party, areas of a single set of ideas, areas in which the free competition of ideas is for the time being proscribed—it is none the less true that in the area of Europe at large, if we regard Europe as a single system, there was never more discussion and competition of ideas than there is to-day? Hardly a State is settled on the lees of ancient custom. Every State is defending its particular *raison d'être* before the bar of Europe, the bar of the world at large. This is not an unhealthy thing. Nor is it, fundamentally, on the tentative and preliminary definition of democracy which we have for the moment adopted, an undemocratic thing.

Shall I now turn to the analysis of dictatorship? It is a Latin word. In order to break the shell of words, which are sometimes like hard Brazil nuts, and to discover the kernel or content of significance which they contain, it is often wise to go back to their first and original meaning. The Roman dictator, as he existed in the Roman Republic from 500 to 200 B.C., was an extraordinary officer of the Republic, who was originally called, and always continued to be called in strict propriety, by the name of *magister populi*—leader of the people, as we might say, or, as a German would say, *Volksführer*. The name, we may note, does not sound unpopular or undemocratic. The bearer of this name was legally appointed, by one of the Consuls, on the strength of a regular decree duly passed by the Senate; he was legally vested with *imperium*, upon his appointment, by a regular law duly passed by one of the *comitia* or assemblies of the people. He had therefore, we may also note, a legal basis or standing. But he was only a temporary officer, for a period of six months or less, and he was only an officer of crisis, to secure the safety of the State. He might secure the safety of the State in one of two ways. He might be appointed, as the Romans said, *rei gerundae causa*—that is to say, as an expeditious organ for the doing of a difficult job, which would generally be a job in the sphere of foreign relations, and would involve the maintenance, or the restoration, of the prestige and honour of the State. Or he might be appointed, as the Romans also said, *seditionis sedandae causa*—or in other words, as a sedative for sedition, in order to settle some inner tension between gentry and populace (or, as a Marxist might say, between capitalism and the proletariat) by a judicious pull to the Right or Left. Now, all these things bear on our modern life, and they raise a number of questions in regard to our modern dictatorships. Are *they* legal, like the old Roman dictatorship, or are they illegal? That is perhaps an academic question. If they begin by a *coup d'état* and a terror, they can easily bring themselves within the four corners of the law which they subsequently proceed to make. Are they temporary, like the old Roman dictatorship, or are they permanent? That is a graver question, to which I must return. For the present I will only say that even if some dictatorships profess a temporary character, as does the Russian dictatorship of the proletariat based on Lenin's philosophy, they also act on the policy that nothing is more permanent than the temporary; and other dictatorships, conceiving themselves *sub specie aeternitatis*, have set their course to ride

Triumphing over Death and Chance and thee, O Time.

There remains still a third question, for our present theme the most momentous of all. Are our modern dictatorships, like the old dictatorship of Rome, compatible with the framework of democracy, or are they, in their essence, antagonistic to popular government and inimical to democracy? We are prone, at any rate in England and in France, to oppose dictatorship to democracy. Is there a real antithesis between the two? Is the modern dictator an incubus on democracy, or a curious, and perhaps pathological, form of democracy itself? Much, of course, will depend on the nature of the dictatorship. If it is a mere brutal force—a sword thrown into the scale and balance of political ideas, or, to alter the metaphor, a sword that cuts instead of solving the Gordian knot of political difficulties—it will be hard to see any democratic tincture in such a form of government. But what if the dictatorship be the dictatorship of a genuine *magister populi*—a real leader of the people, followed heart and soul by a party which contains in itself the dominant current, the majority current, it may even be the only current, of popular opinion? The great dictatorships which count to-day are party dictatorships—in Germany, in Italy, in Russia. Parties have always seemed to be the organs of a democratic system. A majority party which arrogates to itself an exclusive right of existence is indeed a new thing. Hitherto parties have always seemed, by their very nature, to be necessarily plural. But when a single majority party, backed by general majority conviction, is content, and not only content, but eager, to act through a single representative leader, shall we say that democracy is dead, and that we are standing by its coffin?

Ultimately, I believe that the answer is 'Yes'. Ultimately, the essence of democracy is a free process of competition and discussion of political ideas, and therefore of competition and discussion between different political parties; and where this process has stopped, life has ended (because this process is life) and democracy lies dead. But there is also an immediate answer, an answer short of the ultimate, which can be given to our great and mournful question. That immediate answer is a brisk and optimistic 'No'. I wish to pause over that answer. We generally assume, in the current language of political platforms, that what democracy means is that the will of the people must prevail. I do not believe that this is so; and yet I call myself a democrat. I believe that what must prevail is liberty—freedom of the mind, freedom of discussion—the grand dialectic of public debate, in which thought clashes with thought until a reconciling compromise is found which we can all accept because we can all see some little element of our thought, some little reflection of ourselves, in the lineaments which this compromise presents. The mere will of the people can be the greatest enemy to liberty that ever was. It is our English way to love the compromise of conflicting thoughts (for compromise is no ignoble word) rather than the victory of a single will; and that is why we in England are governed by His Majesty's Government and His Majesty's Opposition, acting together in what I have called the grand dialectic of public debate. No Opposition, no democracy: that would be my motto. But let me take the ground we often take on the platform—though I doubt if we really mean it in our hearts—the ground that the will of the people must prevail. On that ground, and upon that basis, we may go on to say that the will of the people may be represented and realised in one of two ways. One way we may call the impersonal way of a system of representative institutions. This is a way which involves the action and the co-operation of four different factors: the factor of a political electorate voting in political constituencies; the factor of a party system, involving at least two parties, and possibly more, which present policies and candidates to the electorate; the factor of a parliament representing political constituencies and organised in parties; the factor of a cabinet representing the majority party (or the majority combination of parties) in that parliament, but confronted and criticised by an opposition representing the minority party, or minority combination of parties. This combination of factors will operate differently in the different States in which it forms the basis of government. It will differ, for example, according as one or another factor predominates in the combination. In France the factor of parliament predominates, and the factor of cabinet has less weight; in England the factor of cabinet is strong, and the factor of parliament seems, in comparison, weak. Again, the combination will differ with differences of the party system. A system of moderate parties, comparatively few in number, will take its place, and claim no more than its place, in the combination. A system of intense and exclusive parties, exacerbated by multiplicity, and accentuated by methods of proportional representation which enable each to claim its pound of flesh, its ounce of flesh, its fraction of an ounce of flesh —such a system may so dominate the combination, and so overbalance the combination, that the whole structure begins to totter.

This brings me to the other way in which the will of the people may be represented and realised. It began to loom up, as you will have guessed, when I came to the end of describing the first way. It is already a fact of our times. Let us look at it frankly, as it now stands before us, and see what it is. It is a form of democracy, or rather it professes to be a form of democracy, in which the will of the people prevails through the emergent leader, the popular dictator, who expresses and incarnates its will. There is a sweeping immediacy about the dictator, a rush from the heart of the people straight to the brain of the leader. The immediacy is not altogether as great as it seems. In the great and typical modern dictatorships there is an intercalated something between the heart and the brain. That something is party, the people's party, the one and only party of the nation, which has elevated the leader and holds him before the people. But if we may eliminate party for the moment—only for the moment, for it is a fact that must never be forgotten in the final account— we may say that dictatorship substitutes the personal fact of direct and immediate representation for the old impersonal system of representative institutions. Dictatorship is a form of democracy—if you will, a pathological form; but that is still to be proved. This is the claim which is made in Italy and Germany alike. Fascism, it is stated

in Signor Mussolini's *La Dottrina del Fascismo*, is the purest
form of democracy, provided that the people be conceived, as it should be, not quantitatively but qualitatively,
and provided, accordingly, that the quality of the people's
will be regarded as actively manifesting itself in the thought
and volition of the Few, or even of the One. A German
professor has recently said much the same of National
Socialism: 'True representation is the personification of
the will of the people in a representative who feels himself
to be one with the people.' These sayings are hardly new.
They are as old as Napoleon. When he addressed the
deputies present at a new year's reception in 1814, he
asked them, 'Do you represent the people? *I* am its representative. Four times have I been summoned by the
nation: four times have I received the votes of five
millions of citizens. I have a right to speak, and you have
none.' The representative popular dictator is not, in himself, a new figure. He is only new in the company which
he keeps. He is new in his association with a party system
which takes the form of a single permitted *Volkspartei.*
He is also new in his association with what is called
corporativism.

These new associates are matters to which I must
presently return. For the moment the point I would
emphasise is that the issue of our times is hardly a simple
issue of democracy *versus* dictatorship. Dictatorship itself
claims the quality of democracy; indeed it claims the
quality of a higher, a more immediate, a more spontaneous
democracy. If we take dictatorships generally, in their
typical modern manifestations, we must rather speak of
the issue engaged as an issue between two types of

democracy—the parliamentary type, with its combination of factors, and the dictatorial type, with its apparent virtue of an immediate and direct simplicity. Stating the issue in these terms, we may proceed to ask why the dictatorial type, at any rate for the time being, is gaining on the parliamentary. The obvious answer to that question is that the defects of the parliamentary type have been the occasion, and the opportunity, for the emergence of the dictatorial. That answer is true enough, and we shall have to discuss it presently; but it is not the whole, or even the greater part, of the real answer. There have been causes at work, profound causes, as well as occasions and opportunities.

We have seen that the old Roman dictators were instituted either *rei gerundae causa*, to serve as expeditious organs for the doing of a difficult job, or *seditionis sedandae causa*. It is the second of these causes which is of particular significance to-day. The tension between capital and labour, present before the War but accentuated by the War, and especially accentuated by the great Russian experiment, has been a profound cause of the dictatorships of the last twelve years. They are counter-dictatorships; they are would-be saviours of society from the first or communist dictatorship established in 1917. I would not say that the communist dictatorship was the root of all evil. Far from it. On the contrary, it was and is a dictatorship seeking to base itself on a genuine democratic foundation of town and village soviets, and professing to go down to the good red earth of immediate popular will. Lenin, as his pamphlet of 1917 on *The State and Revolution* shows, was genuinely concerned to make the proletarian

State a new form of democracy, with the people (in the limited sense of the proletariat) really controlling their representatives, and really dominant not only in legislation, but also in the executive and the judicial spheres. None the less, and whatever we may say of the democratic elements in the theory of Lenin and in the Russian constitution of 1918, there are also two other things to be said. In the first place, the communist dictatorship, in spite of democratic professions, has always been in reality the dictatorship of a party. As such it has helped to provoke, by way of sympathetic contagion, the spread of party dictatorships in other countries. In the second place, the communist dictatorship, by its own inherent nature, was and is the dictatorship of the party of the Left. As such it has furnished the occasion, or at any rate the excuse, by way of reaction and challenge, for the dictatorship of a party of the Right. It was the communist menace which was alleged in Italy in 1922, and in Germany in 1933. It was the fear of that menace (and it hardly matters whether the fear was justified or no, for fear is unreasoning) which rallied support to the Italian and German dictatorships of the Right.

Take next the *rei gerundae causa*; in a word, the need of expeditious solution of urgent national problems, and especially of the problem of restoring national power and prestige. Here time is the argument alleged. In these wild and whirling days we

> always hear
> Time's winged chariot hurrying near,

and how shall we catch up with its flight? The answer is readily given that parliamentary democracy, with its combination of factors, creeks and groans and is left behind; that only dictatorial democracy, with its concentration of decision in one rapid intelligence, can stay the course. That is the plea—a plea as old as our English Stuarts, who buttressed their claims of prerogative (another name for something not unlike dictatorship) on the argument of time and the need of rapid action. It is certainly true that dictatorship can be rapid: it is not equally certain that rapidity is wisdom. Better, perhaps, than the decision of one is the deliberation of many—at any rate if we wish to secure a decision which will be permanent because it is profound, and accepted because it is agreed. But there is a deeper argument than the argument of time behind the dictator who has climed to power *rei gerundae causa*. This is the argument of national power and prestige. Nations, like men, become impatient, and sensitive to the beat of time, when their nerves are frayed, when they feel that they do not count in the world's regard as they ought to count, and that something must be done at once. This was the feeling in Italy and Germany when dictatorship emerged; and this is the feeling which the dictator has satisfied and assuaged. In his person the people can feel that it has quit itself heroically. He has brought honour and freedom. He is a legend, or the author of a legend, on which national pride can feed. The legend may be the Italian legend of the metaphysical *nazione*, raised to new and transcendent heights by the leader whom (as it is written in the preamble to the *Statuto* of the Fascist party) 'the people has recognised by the marks of his will, his force and his work'. Again, it may be the German legend of the racially pure *Volk*, restored to its ancient eminence in Europe by a *Volksführer* of the old heroic pattern. Whatever the legend, it satisfies the national pride, as it is always the function of national legends to do; it is concrete in a person, as national legends generally are, in order to satisfy the deep human instinct for personality; it is attended by emotionalism, enthusiasm, mysticism, the feelings that national legends generally evoke. To the severely rational intelligence, this political mysticism may seem to be, as M. Bérard, classical scholar and minister of education, once said, 'an enthusiastic misconception of realities'. But an enthusiastic misconception of realities may itself be a great reality, which we have to study and understand. And those of us who believe in the rationalism of demo-cracy, conceiving it as the grand dialectic of public debate, must recognise that rationalism is not as warm a thing as emotion, that dialectic is a philosophical quality, and that Plato held (whether rightly or wrongly) that it is impos-sible for a whole people to have the gift of philosophy.

These are some of the profounder causes of modern dictatorship, which has roots, after all, in human needs and sentiments. But human happenings have their occa-sions and opportunities, as well as their profounder causes. The occasion and the opportunity for dictatorial demo-cracy has been provided, as I have said, by the defects of the parliamentary type of democracy. A balanced com-bination of some four different factors, parliamentary democracy needs for its efficiency—we may even say that it needs for its survival—an harmonious system of adjustment, under which each factor takes its place, dis-charges its own specific function, and co-operates duly with the rest. Of the four factors involved—electorate, party, parliament, cabinet—it is the factor of party which has tended to break away, to set itself up as an absolute, and then to introduce the absolute dictator as the organ of its own absoluteness. In their own true nature parties should champion competing ideas which can live side by side; they should present them to the electorate; they should secure their representation in parliament; they should secure their realisation in an organised interplay between cabinet and anti-cabinet, government and opposition. Parties are not armies, penetrated by an *esprit d'armée*, and preparing for a conflict in the nature of a civil war. But that is what, in a great part of Europe, they have tended to become. Instead of serving as organs of the measured debate of opinion, they have begun to wage war *à l'outrance*.

Following the method of Plato when he seeks to trace the decline of the ideal State in the later books of his *Republic*—seeking, in other words, to analyse the logical, rather than the chronological, corruption of parliamentary democracy—we may trace three stages of development. In the first stage, party becomes a self-interested group of politicians eager for the spoils of office and the emoluments of patronage. In the second stage there arises what Signor Mussolini, speaking of the beginnings of Fascism, calls an *anti-partitio*, an anti-party resolved to end the first stage by making itself the sole party and thus restoring the unity and integrity of the State. In this second stage the anti-party, and equally, by way of reaction and in self-defence, the other parties, become totalitarian. In other words, each counts itself an absolute; each professes a *Weltanschauung*, a general, but exclusive, set of social and political ideas; each seeks to provide its members with a whole apparatus of life, for sport, for education, for mutual benefit, for every social purpose; each, in the last resort, turns its adherents into an army, with shirts and military formation. Then comes the third stage, in which the anti-party triumphs. It is a stage best expressed in a phrase of Signor Mussolini, which I have never forgotten since I read it in *La Dottrina del Fascismo*: 'A party which governs a nation totalitarianally is a new historic phenomenon.'

Let us examine this phenomenon. A pathological condition of party has produced a pathological condition of democracy. Party itself has changed. Instead of two or more competing parties seeking to achieve some more or less agreed compromise of ideas, we have a single party clothed in the absolute mantle of totalitarianism. But party is not the only factor which is affected. The three other factors of the combination which constitutes parliamentary democracy, the factors of electorate, parliament and cabinet, must necessarily suffer some corresponding transformation. It is impossible to alter party radically without radically altering the nature of the factors with which it has hitherto been connected. What is the nature of the transformation? We may find the answer in a phrase of M. Joseph Barthélemy: 'The modern dictator is essentially syndicalist.' In other words, the leader of the triumphant totalitarian party adds to his totalitarianism a system of what is now called corporativism. He takes the old syndicalism, tames it into a domesticated animal, and harnesses it under a new name to the chariot of the single-party State. In its ultimate consequences this means the disappearance of the old political electorate of citizens, the old political parliament dealing with general civic issues, the old political government handling these issues in close touch and co-operation with electorate and parliament. In their place we have now the new and apparently two-sided system of the totalitarian-corporative State. On its totalitarian side this means the government of a single party, organised under its own party by-law or *statuto*, and acting through a party leader who, so far as he is responsible, is responsible to a party which he dominates and controls. On its corporative side it means the dissolution of the civic body, with its general civic interests (interests of religion, education, and international affairs, as well as of economics), into so many economic groups, each concerned with its economic interests. And in Italy, at any rate, that dissolution will be total and complete if, as Signor Mussolini announced in November 1933, the very form of an Italian chamber of deputies is to disappear, and its place is to be taken by the National Council of Corporations, composed of the representatives of different economic groups—groups containing both employers and employed, but concerned only with those problems which vex employers and employed.

The modern dictatorship thus stands before us as a Janus with two faces—the one totalitarian, and the other corporative. What shall we say of the logic by which these two are connected? On our own argument, which makes the totalitarian party the primary fact, and the system of corporative grouping something posterior and consequential, we shall be tempted to say that the logic is that of *divide et impera*. In other words, the *imperium* of the party will best be secured if the body of the nation is divided into economic groups, and each is led to concentrate its interest on the economic issues peculiar to itself. But another explanation is possible; and it is an explanation given by the philosophers of Fascism. According to this explanation the system of co-operative grouping, though it may have come later in time, is really the primary fact. Corporativism is the one true way of solving the social problem which is the problem of our times. Put employers and employed together in corporations—corporations (and here I quote from a resolution presented to the Italian Council of Corporations on 13 November 1933) which under the ægis of the State discipline the productive forces in view of the wealth, the political power and the well-being of the people—do this, and then you solve the social problem which is set to us by the modern Sphinx. But even if corporativism be regarded as the ultimate goal, I would ask you to notice that you must first of all have the ægis of the State, the State totalitarianally governed by a single party. Totalitarianism may be a means, but it is a necessary and indispensable means. It was on this basis, I imagine, that Signor Mussolini declared to the Council of Corporations, on the day following its resolution (14 November), that 'for a full, complete and integral corporativism it is necessary to have only one political party and a unitary State'.

We have looked at the present: what shall we say of the future? Here I return to a question of which I gave notice before, the final question I have to raise. Are modern dictatorships temporary, like the old Roman dictatorship, or will they be permanent? Has parliamentary democracy finally disappeared from Europe in the region east of the

Rhine and south of the Baltic; or is it a seed maturing in the deep underground of the lives of nations, which will yet burst into a new growth? Experience has already shown that modern dictatorships can last, and are likely to last, for many years. The communist dictatorship has already lasted for a longer period than the rule of Napoleon; and the Fascist dictatorship in Italy is already adolescent. No revolutionary movement, attempting to answer force by force, is likely to overset the dictator's throne, unless, indeed, such a movement should receive the adhesion of the army. In these days of scientific inventions which are all at the disposal of the government—wireless, telephones, aeroplanes, fleets of lorries and motor-cars—the dictator can always detect in advance, and nip in the bud, all revolutionary attempts. The decline or collapse of dictatorship, if it comes at all, is likely to come from within. There are a number of internal factors which seem to be insecure. In the first place, an essential feature of most of our modern dictatorships is personality—the single dominating heroic personality. Can we count on the permanent presence of such personality? What is to happen if the person on whom all hopes are fixed should crack under the strain of perpetual racking decision? What is to happen if he should ossify in his policy, and lose touch with the living movement of national life? Parliamentary democracy can meet this danger of ossification, inherent in all governments, by a new election and a new choice; but that way is foreclosed to dictatorship, which must either turn of itself with the turning tide or take up arms against it. There is still a further question which arises from this essential feature of personality. What is to happen when the single person, in the natural course of events, disappears at last from the stage? Here there arises the great problem of the succession to the dictator's throne; and that, we may say, is a problem which still awaits solution. In Russia, indeed, a solution seems to have been found. Stalin has succeeded to Lenin—Amurath to Amurath. The Communist party in Russia has been able to throw up a new personality, and the Fascist party in Italy may be able to do the like. The Grand Council of the party, under a law of 1929, can make and keep up to date a list of names to be presented to the Crown, in the event of a vacancy, for the office of party leader and chief of the government. This brings us to a second factor and a second essential feature in the structure of modern dictatorships—the single totalitarian party. Even if this factor can solve the problem of the succession to the office of dictator, is it itself a secure and established factor, which we can expect to endure permanently? We may admit that it is likely to endure while the wave of emotion endures by which it is sustained—the emotion of national pride and prestige, the emotion of the national legend, the emotion of the metaphysical nation, conceived as an organism with a higher being that transcends and subsumes the being of persons and groups, the emotion of the pure racial *Volk*. But assume that the emotion subsides and that the passion of national pride and prestige becomes satisfied, or simply jaded, according to that law of satiety to which all human emotions and passions are subject. In that event, national feeling may cease to sustain the single party and the single person in whom its ideal is incarnate. Internal problems of national

life—problems within the gates, problems of social justice
and social equality—may begin to arrest attention and
produce divisions of opinion. Where can the divisions be
debated, and where can some compromise be found?
That brings us to a third factor and a third essential feature
in the structure of modern dictatorships—the idea and
feature of corporativism, expressed in some sort of corporative chamber. Can such a chamber, divided into
economic groups, ever be an arena of national debate on
great national issues which transcend the interests and the
capacities of such groups? Must there not be an ultimate
return, if ever the single party cracks into two or more
divisions, towards a political parliament in which, and in
which alone, such parties can act and vote? Either the
political debate of parties in a political parliament, or the
civil war of parties in a stricken field. Is there any third
choice?

In the light of what I have just said, I cannot envisage
the permanence of modern dictatorships in their present
form, except perhaps in Russia, which is a problem by
itself. They must evolve still further, in one direction or
another. In my imagination I can see two opposite directions. One would lead forward to something like the old
Roman Empire—the rule of a Cæsar, backed by an army
(which in this age would be a party army) and sanctified
by Cæsar-worship. But in our modern days of publicity
we can hardly expect a return to Cæsar-worship, though
things are happening which look curiously like the old
adoration. Another direction would lead backwards, to
something like the old system of parliamentary democracy. I confess that I expect some backward return; but

I do not think that it will be a return to parliamentary democracy of our West-European pattern. I should rather expect the dictator to leave his permanent mark, at any rate in Germany, in the shape of a strong presidential executive, somewhat after the American pattern, with a political parliament debating and tugging at his side. That may be an idle dream. But the executive tradition is strong in the country of Frederick the Great and William I; in some way or other I should expect to see it maintained. In Italy, too, where the Roman tradition of administration is still alive, I should expect to see something similar. Our English tradition of the sovereignty of Parliament is not necessarily right for Mittel-Europa.

But will our English tradition last in England itself? Is parliamentary democracy, with its combination of four factors, safe on its throne in Western Europe—in France and Spain, in Belgium and Holland, in the Scandinavian countries by the waters of the Atlantic and the North Sea? I shall only speak of England. Here the answer depends on the line which parties take. The spirit of party is the crux of the matter. Are our parties resolved to be absolutes, to become totalitarian, to urge the argument of time ('now or never our principles must be realised, in all their totality, by the use of emergency powers')? Are they resolved to profess and follow the theory that they are mutually exclusive opposites? If the Right wing of Conservatism should dominate the Conservative party, and the Left wing of Socialism should dominate Labour, we are in danger of that consummation; and that consummation will mean dictatorship or counter-dictatorship. Or can our parties consent to give and take; can they have patience, knowing that Time gives time to all his children; can each party honour and take over the main lines of the legislation of its predecessor in office, recognising the continuity of national life; can all parties agree to differ without ceasing to agree on the main foundations and principles of an old but not antiquated constitution, which has done and is still able to do great service to the cause of human rights and liberty? If the answer be 'Yes', we can go forward in hope, welcoming the alternation and succession of parties in office, because each has its contribution to bring to the common cause, and each must have its chance of making its contribution. But everything, I repeat, depends on the spirit of party. And since the spirit of a party depends on the nature and inspiration of its leadership, I would add that the burden of responsibility laid on our English leaders to-day is the gravest of burdens that men can well bear. If they get flustered and hurried by the sense of the pressure of time; if they accentuate the principles of their party to the extremity of their logic; if they exaggerate their party programme into an imperative and exclusive gospel, in the haste of their hearts and under the contagion of foreign example, we shall go the way that others have gone, and end in a party dictatorship if not in a party dictator.

I can understand party passion; I can understand party haste for some immediate divine event; I can understand party conviction of the absolute righteousness of the party cause. But patience and perspective are great goddesses in human affairs—patience and perspective, and especially perspective. If we can keep things in perspective—ourselves, our policies, our party—we shall keep our own heads, and we shall allow the other side to keep their heads on their shoulders. Revolutions come, and heads fall, when patience and perspective have been forgotten. We *may* lose the battle of parliamentary democracy in England for the time being, though that would not be my own prophecy. We *may*, short of that, have to modify the combination of factors which makes up our system of parliamentary democracy, though I see no particular modification which I desire, or even expect, except in matters of detail, such as the composition of the Second Chamber, the procedure of the First Chamber (which is at some points antiquated and cumbrous), the methods of voting in elections, and other similar matters. But there is one thing which I believe will never be finally lost, in England or elsewhere, on a long-time view of the nature of political society and the necessary mode of its operation. The thing I mean is government by discussion—government by the free competition of different political ideas, by the process of debate between those ideas, by the method of adjusting competition and debate in a compromise which reconciles differences. No form of government can be true to the process of social thought unless it proceeds on that basis. My fundamental belief is a belief in government by discussion—free, patient, rational discussion. This to me is the highest form of democracy, when a free people, freely thinking its different thoughts, freely expresses them by different parties, freely debates them in a freely elected parliament, and freely reconciles them by the free interplay and co-operation of parties—government and opposition, cabinet and anti-cabinet—in such a parliament. Government by discussion, by debate, by dialectic, this to me is the true democracy; and it is a thing which is inevitable when the mind of man, duly educated to his high nature of a rational being, is acting in its true and natural mode of operation. You may say that I believe in government by dialectic rather than in government by Demos. I reply that the Demos to which I look forward will necessarily love dialectic, the grand dialectic of public debate. 'Give me the liberty to know, to utter, and to argue freely according to conscience, above all liberties.' So said Milton. I can say nothing better, or as good; and I have nothing more to say.

IV

THE SOCIAL BACKGROUND OF RECENT POLITICAL CHANGES

Delivered at the Institute of Sociology, London, 12 February 1936

I t is not necessarily Marxianism to interpret political changes in the light of social factors. What is peculiar to Marxianism is the tendency to interpret political changes in no other light. As long ago as Aristotle, we find political forms and political changes ascribed to social causes. Speaking of political forms, Aristotle notes that 'oligarchy exists when men of property have the government in their hands; democracy in the opposite case, when the indigent, and not the men of property, are the rulers'. Speaking of political changes, or, as he calls them, revolutions, he notes particularly the changes or revolutions which come from the increase, or the decrease, of one of the social factors in the State. 'A State has many parts, of which some one may grow imperceptibly...revolutions arise from this cause in democracies as well as in other forms of government.' If we follow Aristotle in seeking to explain political changes, we shall thus take into account, of course among other causes, the cause which is to be found in these imperceptible growths of social factors, and in the subsequent shifting of what may be called the social balance. The same lesson was taught, still more imperatively, by one of our English political thinkers in the seventeenth century. James Harrington, in the introduction to his *Oceana* of 1656, which he dedicated to Cromwell, laid down the principle, 'As is the proportion or balance of Dominion, or property in land, so is the nature of the Empire'—that is to say, of the government. Confining his attention to land, the great and visible form of wealth in his day and generation, he argued that the Crown was now impoverished, the middle classes were wealthy, and a commonwealth or republic must therefore take the place of monarchy. 'Let the King come in', he prophesied (according to a story told by Aubrey) on the eve of the Restoration, 'and call a parliament of the greatest cavaliers in England, so they be men of estates, and let them sit but seven years, they will all turn Commonwealth's men.' It would take a good deal of argument to decide how far Harrington was right, and how far he was wrong, in this prophecy. There was certainly a Whig party established by 1675, and there was certainly a Whig Revolution in 1688. On the other hand, there was a contemporary of James Harrington who also based his philosophy on the middle classes, and who reached what seems to be a diametrically opposite conclusion. This was Thomas Hobbes. He argued that what the middle classes wanted, *sua si bona norint*—if only they knew their own interests—was a good strong government which policed their property. He put that argument definitely in an appeal to the middle classes—perhaps it would better be called a definite scolding of the middle classes; and it is not a bad answer to Harrington.

If we sought to argue in the most modern and up-to-date terms, we might substitute Pareto for Aristotle and

Harrington, and talk about 'the circulation of élites' as the true social background of political change. Perhaps it is better to argue in nobody's terminology, but to begin by defining the terms which we are using ourselves. On that basis we must notice the width of meaning of the term 'social background'. Instinctively, and at the first blush, we interpret that term in reference to the distribution of property, the system of classes determined (or mainly determined) by that distribution, and the social balance between the different factors in that system. This is the interpretation followed, in different ways, by Aristotle and Harrington, as it is also followed, in his own peculiar way, by the Marxian. But there is also a larger interpretation of the idea of social background, which befits the sociologist, and indeed must necessarily be followed by the sociologist. On that interpretation we shall include in the social background of political changes not only the distribution of property, the system of classes, and the shifting of the balance of classes, but a number of other factors. In the first place, we shall include the mere size and mass of population—in itself, and regardless of the particular way in which it is distributed in different classes. The mere number of the population is in itself a social factor of the first magnitude. A vastly increased population, such as the nineteenth century produced, will ultimately entail problems of political organisation which involve changes of political method—new forms, for example, of party machinery, to manipulate the new numbers: new forms of the general drill and discipline of life, to regulate the new movement of great crowds along all routes. The factor of population, in all its ramifications

—not only internal, but also external, and in its bearing on emigration and general expansion—is one of the greatest factors in the social background of political change. There are other factors which have also to be counted. There is, for example, the increase and the speeding of communications—both physical communication by new methods of transport, and mental communication by telegraph, telephone, and wireless. These things affect and alter the pace of politics; and an alteration of the pace of politics is already a political change, which may bring other changes in its train. Again, the alteration of the family may produce alterations in the State. If the family becomes less of a solid unit, and less responsible for its members, the State will be charged with greater responsibilities and become more of a paternal authority. It is not always the encroachment of the State which diminishes the area of the family: the reverse may be the case, and the shrinkage of the family may involve the increase of the State. Similarly, the development of education, in itself a form of social change and an alteration of the social background, may involve political consequences and changes. If, for example, there is a large resort to the Universities, and if the result is the production of an unemployed intelligentsia, or of an intelligentsia not employed in the ways and on the standards which its members feel entitled to expect, there will arise a new social factor which is particularly likely to make political demands and to precipitate political changes.

Before we turn to examine the political effects of the social background in this broader and more general sense, we may pause to enquire whether we can trace, behind any of the recent political changes in Europe, social causes of that more specific character which we associate with the conception of class. Class is a dangerous word. There is hardly any community which can show a definite system of classes, or even anything approaching such a system. Occupations and professions are definite things, but class is a term of rhetoric rather than a term of art. When we speak of class-feelings and class-movements, we are postulating a unit, and a unity of that unit, which reality seldom warrants. Even the working class, which is most definitely a class, is a collection of different feelings and different movements; and when we turn to the middle class, or the middle classes, we are turning to something which is even more indefinite. None the less, there is a sense in which we say that Fascism and National Socialism are movements of the middle class, including in that term partly the members of the professions and those who expect to enter the professions, partly the independent artisan and the shopkeeper, and partly the middle interests in the world of agriculture. It is difficult to test such a generalisation in any scientific way. We should need, for that purpose, a social census of the membership of each movement concerned; and even that would not give us sufficient data unless we could weigh, in some way, the relative influence of its different sections. There was an occasion, about 1921, when the Secretary of the Fascist party in Italy gave an account of the social composition of one half of his party; and it is significant that the greater part of that half—some 90,000 out of a total of 150,000—could be classed as independent or professional. The origins and the careers of the leaders are another index. It is true that a victorious party, once in power, recruits all sorts of adherents, who follow the banner of success: it is also true that, once in power, it may adjust its policy to the exigencies of its new position, and incorporate plans and aims which do not belong to its own beginnings. That only makes it the more necessary to go back to the party beginnings in order to understand the social background from which it came and the social needs and desires which impelled it to seek political change. If we go back in that way to the origins of National Socialism, we shall find that, like Italian Fascism, it appealed to the middle interests of society, severely shaken and battered by the hurricanes of the currency, and barred from its hopes of professional advancement by a régime in which posts seemed destined wholly for another class. One of the original twenty-five points of the party programme demanded the creation and maintenance of a sound middle class, the socialisation of the large stores and their rental at low cost to small traders, and special consideration for such traders in purchases made on behalf of the State. Another, addressed to the middle interest in agriculture, demanded land reform suitable to the national needs, the enactment of a law for the expropriation of land for social purposes, the abolition of rent on land, and the prevention of all kinds of speculation in land.

Why should there have been this insurgence of the middle classes in Germany and Italy? We are driven back on a simple cause—the convulsion of the War. The War had shaken irreparably the position of the governing class, or perhaps we had better say the governing element, under the shelter of which the middle classes had gone their way and preserved their respectability and their self-respect. A new governing element had emerged, or threatened to emerge, from the ranks of the working classes who followed the creed of socialism. The new governing element imperilled their advancement in the service of the State—a service which bulks more largely on the Continent than it does with us in the prospect of a career; and in any case, it imperilled the maintenance of self-respect. A country which is ready to accept and respect a labour government must have gone a long way in the recognition of the principle that 'a man's a man for a' that'. It must also have gone a long way in the recognition, and the practical application, of the principle that the permanent service of the State is divorced from all social favour, and is freely open to all capacity, irrespective of social convention. If this way has not been travelled, the imminence of a labour government will convey a double threat to the middle class—a threat to its self-respect and sense of personal dignity: a threat to its hope of advancement and prospects of a career. The insurgence of the middle classes is the answer to that double threat.

It is difficult to understand contemporary Italy and Germany without remembering Russia, and without reflecting on the different development of Russia. Russia supplied the bugbear which served to frighten millions into the fold of a warm and comfortable middle-class State. But why did Russia herself, under the impact of a similar cause—the convulsion of the War—follow a line of development so peculiar, and so different from that of other States? The answer is naturally found in the difference of the social background of Russia. An amorphous but plastic society of little farming communities had long been shaped by a governing bureaucracy, with a large foreign element in its composition, and by a landed nobility. The system had been shaken by war in 1905: it was finally destroyed by war in 1917. What was to take its place? There was only one social element which offered itself. This was the element of industrial labour in the towns and factory settlements which had grown up in Russia during the latter half of the nineteenth century. There was no other social element of sufficient volume and strength— no middle element of the professions, or in the country-side, or in the world of trade and business, in which, from the eighteenth century onwards, a number of foreign interests, English among the rest, had always been mainly active. The element of industrial labour—a minority, but an active minority, with definite objects and a definite leadership—surged to the front. The amorphous but plastic society found a new control. The ideals of industrial labour became dominant; and the little farming communities were shaped into accordance with them.

If there were time and space, the analysis of the social background in terms of class, and of the effects of that background in producing political change, might be carried further. We might speak, for example, of the resurgence of the old peasant culture in the Danubian lands; of the development of peasant proprietorship, since the War, in large areas of those lands; and of the political consequences of that development in the States in which it has taken place. The terms of property and of class which belong to urbanised, industrialised, and commercialised communities are not proper to agricultural communities; and it is dangerous to import any common scheme into the interpretation of the varied face of Europe. But it is time to turn to those broader aspects of social life and the social background which still remain for our consideration. Beyond the play of property and class, there is also the play of other forces. There is the great population: there is the great change of communications; there is the stirring of society and the social process by a new diffusion of education. Can we trace the effects of these causes—these elements of our contemporary social background—in any of the political changes of our times?

One of the political portents of the present time—perhaps the greatest of them—is the magnification of party. When Bryce published his *Modern Democracies* in 1921—how long ago that seems, and how far have parties, and politics generally, travelled in fifteen years—he was alarmed by the growth of parties and party spirit, and anxious to find checks to their growth. The parties of our day are giants to what they were when he wrote. In Russia, Germany, and Italy, however much they may be divided otherwise, there is one common fundamental political fact. That fact is the integration of the State in a party, the domination of the State by a party—a single party; a party of a closed membership, though the membership may run to two or three millions; a party which gives its members a special status, dignity, and privilege. There are differences between the formal position of party in any one of these States and its formal position in others. In Russia the Communist party is formally separate from the State; and though its members actually inspire all the action of the State, the party itself, *de jure*, has no lot or part in the Constitution. In Italy, the Fascist party is a part of the Constitution: it has a formal right, under the law of May 1928, to take a legal part in the conduct of parliamentary elections: it has also a formal right, under another law of December 1928, to give its advice on constitutional changes—including, under that head, 'international treaties which involve a renunciation of the acquisition of territories'—and to suggest to the Crown the names of persons for the office of Prime Minister. But these differences, important as they are, do not abolish a fundamental identity. Formally, or informally, a single organised party, of a closed membership, controls the destinies of these countries. Not content with its own membership of adults, the party proceeds to incorporate youth, adolescence, childhood, and even infancy, in its ranks. In Italy, for example, as it was announced in the early months of 1936, a pre-Balilla of boys under six is now being added to the Balilla for children from six to fourteen, the Avanguardisti for adolescents from fourteen to eighteen, and the Young Fascists for youths from eighteen to twenty-one.

What is the social background from which this portent comes? Why has this factor of party, once a voluntary association parallel to other voluntary associations, and moving like them within the framework and shelter of the State, shot into the foreground, captured the State and proceeded to organise the whole of life? It is a difficult and complicated question. But there are some factors in recent social development which suggest something of an answer. In a great population men diversify their lives by taking 'sides'. They may simply espouse an athletic side, and become the fans of a team. In the circus of the great and populous Constantinople there were already Blues and Greens fourteen hundred years ago; and the Blues and Greens, from being circus-factions, spilled over into politics and shook the throne of Justinian. There is no 'side' more fascinating than the political, and nothing more calculated to diversify life, especially if it be organised with pomp and banners and uniform. As soon as the electorate increased in size and became the electorate of a great population, the party organiser was at work. In England the second Reform Bill of 1867 was followed at once by the Liberal Caucus and Mr Schnadhorst; and an eruption and insurgence of party seemed imminent, particularly when Lord Randolph Churchill, in the early eighties of last century, threw himself into the task of galvanising the National Union of Conservative Associations into a fervent activity. But in a homogeneous country, accustomed to conduct disputes between sides by rules of the game, or at any rate professing that object, the fervour of a party side, however hotly it boils for a time, tends ultimately towards a moderate temperature. Where society is less homogeneous, the temper of the side prevails. It is this prevalence of the temper of the side which has been so marked a feature of so many continental countries in the post-War years. Nowhere, perhaps, was it more marked than in Germany. The party side became a total focus of life. The party creed developed into a general *Weltanschauung*: the party sought to provide for its members the whole apparatus of life—mutual benefit, education, sport, military exercise, whatever the mind can crave. When parties thus become total, there is, in the last resort, only room for one. And when one total party triumphs, the State goes—or rather, as the current phrase runs, it becomes 'totalitarian', which is only to say that it becomes the subject and the plaything of the total party.

No doubt it is questions of property and the interests of social classes which help to precipitate parties. But they are not the only questions. What makes the side, and maintains the side, may be primarily questions of national position and national prestige, even if questions of property and the interests of social classes are also mixed in the tissue. In any case, the problem before us is not so much that of the grounds on which parties are formed, as that of the causes which give them—whatever the grounds on which they are formed—the intensity, the totality, the dominance which they nowadays tend to assume. These characteristics will not readily develop except in a heterogeneous society; but the fact of social difference and social cleavage is not, in itself, sufficient to explain them. We must also take into account the great population. We must equally take into account the new powers and processes of manipulating emotion which are furnished by the multiplication of communications. The modern leader, flying by aeroplane, is ubiquitous. His voice can become familiar to millions over the wireless: his face and his mannerisms are diffused to millions by the film. The power of organising sides has been vastly increased by the mechanical development of our civilisation. It is somewhat terrifying to reflect upon the repercussions of these mechanical developments on politics. On the one hand, they make it easy to assemble gigantic combinations, tuned in eye and ear to a dominant mode. On the other hand, when once such a combination has been established, they make it difficult for any vestige of opposition even to appear. The tendency to take sides defeats itself; it ends by producing a solitary side, which, because it is solitary, is not a side. One can hardly imagine a modern Garibaldi. He would be defeated at once in a modern world where light is such that every movement is instantaneously visible and sound is such that every stirring is immediately audible. He would be overwhelmed at once by an instantaneous concentration of aeroplanes.

If we may count in the social background the two factors which have just been mentioned—the factor of numbers and the factor of their methods of communication—we begin to see more of the far-spread roots of recent political change. But these factors are only a part, and a tolerably simple part, of the whole matter. Shaken societies are seeking to reform themselves. Some substitute has to be found for the old governing stratum and the old governing elements. Where this has happened, men are going through an experimental stage, in which a party combination offers itself, or obtrudes itself, as a substitute. In the period of effervescence, the party combination reaches down into the depths for its leaders and its adherents. The young men from the schools and the Universities, the teachers and the journalists, many sorts and conditions of men, see a rising star. Both those who wish to receive and those who wish to give and to make an offering rally to the cause of party. It was an impressive thing to one who talked with the young men in a German University, two years ago, to see how their hopes were set on party. Not advancement in a profession, not entry into the professional service of the State, not a parliamentary career (how could there be one?), but enlistment in the party, and a happy combination of personal advancement and service to the community through such enlistment—these were the terms in which the eager and ambitious were thinking. The party is at once a career and a dedication: it unlocks the doors: *per me si va nella citta godente.* We cannot realise the zest of party unless we also realise that party seems an entrance to a new world, a new America, in which careers abound and jobs spring brightly from the soil like wild flowers.

In conditions such as these there is something apocalyptic, something (if the word may be permitted) 're-vivalistic', in the glorified party of our days. Those who saw the great crowds—moving by their grandeur, and yet also, in their mass, terrible—which assembled on the funeral day of our late King will understand the sense of apocalypse and the feeling of revival. This is what the great population and the whirring shuttle of its communications can produce. It is a sort of mysticism, supra-rational or infra-rational, according as you choose to regard it. With us this mysticism seems to gather about existing institutions, and especially the monarchy. That is the lesson of May 1935 and January 1936. Will it endure, and what are the forms which it will eventually take? I do not know: I only hold my breath. Elsewhere, with existing institutions less stable and less magnetic, the mysticism has gathered round new centres, and has precipitated itself in mystical parties. There is the centre of class, and the mystical party of Communism. There is the centre of race, and the mystical party of the National Socialists. There is the centre of the 'national organism', as it appears in the very first article of the Italian Charter of Labour, and there is the mystical party of Fascism, engaged in what the Greeks called *proskynesis* at the feet of the organism. Every centre has its incarnation in a hero: each mystical party has its Duce, or Führer, or, as he is more modestly called in Russia, its Secretary. When the great population swarms, it must have its queen-bee. When the side emerges, it must cluster round the emergent leader; and you will have what I cannot but call—vulgarly, but I think truly—the cult of the 'boosted hero'.

When one thinks of such things, and when one looks at the social background in this fierce light, the future cannot but appear cloudy. Perhaps the great population will decline and dwindle: perhaps, in the days of our great-grandchildren, there will be vacant spaces—abundant room—airy interstices in what was once a warm and serried mass. Perhaps the speed of the whirring shuttle will ease its strain; perhaps we shall be trained, by a process of adaptation, to its stress, and no longer be excited and dazzled by the whirr. Meanwhile, we live in the age in which we live. We have to understand it in order to master it: self-knowledge is the only way to self-control. To understand our age in terms of economics—if by economics we mean the distribution of property and the system of classes—is to understand it only in part. There are other things also afoot. Our numbers; our communications and contacts; the temper and tempo of life which spring from our numbers and contacts—these also count, and count very greatly.

Take, for example, the sphere of the external relations of States. Hitherto we have been looking at the State 'at home'—the State in its own multifarious and crowded house. But suppose we imagine it walking abroad, travelling, prospecting—like that old race which anthropologists call the Prospectors. What will it find? Still more important—what will it *want* to find? Well, it will want some things which are definitely economic. It will want emigration areas; and it will find the gates of the old areas shut, except for a little wicket-gate labelled 'Quota'. It will want areas, or it will think it wants areas, for the supply of new materials; and it will find a world pre-empted and pre-occupied. But is this all it will want, and are these the essential things which, in its heart of hearts, it really wants? If we are thinking of the party State—the State with the social background and the temper of life of which we have just been speaking—the answer will be 'No'. The background of its foreign policy will be more than economic, and it will transcend considerations of emigration areas and areas for the supply of raw materials. Because such a State is a 'side' at home, it will move as a 'side' when it goes abroad. Its fundamental consideration will be, in a word, prestige. It will desire to count. These great self-conscious populations move out into the world with their self-consciousness upon them. That they should argue their case in terms of any international system, or at the bar of any international organ, is already for them a surrender of the thing for which they are contending— the respect they desire to impose and the prestige they desire to assert. They may use economic terms; but they seek a super-economic reality, which is none the less a reality for them because it is an intangible matter of status and consequence. There is nothing very new about the desire of States for status and consequence. The old dynastic States had that desire. The new thing about the new party States is that their desire for status and consequence is not the calculation of diplomats but the mysticism of masses. The Duce of Fascist Italy is different from Bismarck; and a place in the sun means more to-day than it meant—or at any rate it means something different from what it meant—thirty years ago.

My theme is infinite, but your patience is finite. I wish I could speak to you about the social background not only of political change, but also of political stability. There are, after all, some countries in which such a background seems to exist—countries which have found, as it were, their form: which are somehow one: which can reconcile the unity of the State with the differences of political parties, and the unity of society with the heterogeneity of its classes. I will not seek to penetrate their secret: I will only comfort myself, and you, by reflecting that all is not for the worst in the worst of all possible worlds. I will add another reflection. Those of us who learned our history at the end of the nineteenth century were taught to think of the unification of Germany and of Italy as if they were processes that had been already achieved in 1870. We now see that they were *not* achieved. They are still being achieved. The Führer and the Duce are the new Bismarck and the new Cavour of a new unification—a unification under the new and troublous conditions of a new social background. If a final unification proves to be the outcome of these coils and perturbations in Italy and Germany, they too may find the secret. We, who were unified long ago, cannot but deplore what to us are sad

excesses of unitarian zeal—nowhere sadder, because nowhere more calculated and more doctrinaire, than they
are in Germany, with its passion for the one Reich which
is also one race and one religion. But just because we
were unified long ago, in days when the majestic
Henry VIII and the masterful Cromwell did their work
upon us, we must also acknowledge that unity has to be
won before stability can be found. Besides (and this is a
sobering thought), have we ourselves yet found our final
unity? Is the warfare accomplished? Or is there still a
higher unity to be attained—the unity of a comradely
society and of 'joy in widest commonalty spread'? One
of the features in the policy of the authoritarian unifiers of
our days is that by party organisation of adults, and by
ancillary organisation of youth, and by a supplementary
organisation of leisure for the common and commonly
shared activities of *Kraft durch Freude* and *Dopolavoro*, they
pull the strings of community taut and draw together all
sorts and conditions in common bonds. Their political
zeal for unity works back on the social background and
produces a zeal for social unity. Perhaps this zeal for social
unity is but a by-product of politics: certainly the unity
achieved is an imposed unity. But we have also something
to learn; and these things are a challenge to us. In our
different way, and by our different methods of voluntary
action, we too have to work back on our social background. We, who are free and equal citizens under the
law by virtue of our political system, have now to carry
the spirit of our citizenship into the social depths. If the
social background throws up political changes, and moves
and convulses the political mass, is it not also true that a

system of politics, if it commands our trust and satisfies our moral sense, will by its own logic be driven—no, I would rather say move—towards the making of social change and the quickening of the social mass? The political system is not a mere barometer or seismograph which simply registers social pressure and social movement. It is also, so far as it is based on abiding values, and wherever it is so based, a mariner's compass or a lighthouse. It need not 'bend with the remover to remove'. It can ease and adjust social pressures: it can even initiate and guide social movements.

V

THE CORPORATIVE STATE

An essay written originally in 1934, after a visit to Rome and Vienna, and revised in 1936

We English, not a very thoughtful people, sometimes throw off ideas, without being aware of it, which afterwards go on, as the French say, *faire fortune*. We threw off, for instance, the idea of parliamentarianism; or rather (for our primary concern is generally to get something done, and to think about it afterwards) we hit on a way of doing things which could be, and was, elaborated into that idea. In the same way we seem to have thrown off, in a fit of absence of mind, the idea of corporativism. The suggestion may seem paradoxical. It is a wise father who knows his own child; at any rate we English have not always had the wisdom to recognise the children of our own empirical thought. But it is certainly true that the Whitley Report suggested in 1917 (primarily with a view to getting something done on immediate questions, such as those connected with demobilisation and the restoration of the Trade Union rules and customs suspended during the War) a system of Joint Standing Industrial Councils in the several industries, composed of representatives of employers and employed. And it is certainly true that the idea thus thrown off, which among us has come to be known as 'Whitleyism', and has made no very great fortune, is like the idea of 'corporativism'. But it is also true that analogy is no proof of affiliation; and having brought on the scene this English idea—which we have curiously christened, in our usual manner, by the name of the chairman of the committee in which it was brought to birth—we may dismiss it into the background, as a dubious case of presumptive parentage, and turn to the *corporazione*, or guild, or vocational group, which has been busy for some years in Italy, and also, of late, in Portugal and Austria. (May I say in passing how fascinating it was, on the May Day of 1934, when the new Austrian constitution was promulgated, to sit in front of the Town Hall in Vienna, and to see the vocational groups—*die berufständische Hauptgruppen*—walking in visible procession before me, with their emblems at their head? When I saw my brother-professors, in the group of 'the free professions', I had a sudden access of group-feeling such as seldom visits my old-fashioned individualistic mind, trained in the school of English Nonconformity and English Liberalism, and always haunted by a solemn and inescapable sense of individual responsibility.)

Corporativism to-day has its principal home in Italy. An Italian *corporazione* (perhaps it is more accurate to translate the word into our English 'guild', but the word 'corporation' springs naturally to the pen) is *not* a corporation, in our English sense of the word. It is not corporate; it does not possess a legal personality; it is not an institution of private law. It is a public-law 'organ of the administration of the State'. It is a State-created and State-controlled union of the Trade Unions (or 'syndicates') of employers and employed, in some determinate branch of production, industrial or agricultural. The Trade Unions which it unites, if and provided that they are legally recognised—and to be legally recognised they must consist of members who are sympathisers with the Fascist régime—*are* corporations, and *do* possess juridicial personality under the system of private law. We may thus define the *corporazione* as a non-corporate public-law body (a single body, or *corpus*, uniting two partners in one flesh), which is formed when the State draws together, in some branch of economic activity, representatives from the corporate private-law associations concerned with the affairs of that branch. 'A corporation', it was stated in a decree of 1 July 1926, 'unites the syndicated national organisations of the different factors of production (employers, and workers both intellectual and manual) in a determinate branch of production.' Formed by the State, and acting as an organ of the State, the corporation serves the purposes of the State by promoting the interests of the nation which is 'integrally realised' in the State. It is 'an instrument which, under the ægis of the State, disciplines the productive forces in view of the wealth, the political power, and the well-being of the Italian nation'. The discipline which it exercises is intended to secure economic peace, by the 'collective regulation of the economic relations' between the two parties engaged in production; it is also intended to promote economic prosperity, by the 'unitarian regulation of production' with a view to its greater efficiency. In a word, the corporation is at once a system of conciliation and a method of rationalisation. But in both its aspects, we must always remember, it is always an organ of the State. In this respect, and on this point, which is crucial, corporativism differs essentially from Whitleyism. The Joint Standing Industrial Councils proposed in the Whitley Report were commended to

Employers' Associations and Trade Unions by the State; but if they were commended, they were never, in any way, commanded. Their institution was left to the voluntary activity of the bodies concerned. Their subsequent action was equally left to the same sphere of voluntary or social activity. The Whitley Council belongs to Society. The *corporazione* belongs to the State. This is a fundamental difference.

The theory of the corporation was enunciated in Italy in 1926, and it has been carried into effect by successive laws and decrees down to the law of 13 January 1934, 'on the formation and functions of corporations'. But the origin of the theory goes back earlier than 1926. Before the War, some twenty-five years ago, Signor Mussolini had already begun to take a lively interest in syndicalism, as an alternative—and perhaps a preferable alternative—to socialism. Syndicalism proper means a revolt against the State, or at any rate a turning away from the State: it means that the workers in each branch of industry assume for themselves a sovreignty over their branch, and manage by themselves the activities of their branch. At first attracted by this philosophy, the thought of the Duce eventually travelled beyond it. Passing through the crucible of historic contingencies and political experience, syndicalism was modified—we may almost say domesticated—into corporativism. In the first place the State, which the syndicalist banishes, was set in the centre and made the mainspring. In the second place the controlling group in each branch of industry, which on the theory of syndicalism is a single group of the workers only, became a double group including employers as well as workers.

On this basis, and from these origins, a new philosophy emerged, which could pit itself equally against Liberalism and Socialism, and claims to transcend them both. It was a philosophy which regarded the married vocational group—married, in the sense that capital and labour had become consorts—as the true and essential social unit. In place of the Socialistic conception of warring classes—in place of the Liberal conception of free competitive individuals—there stood the Corporative conception of vocational groups, each of them harmonious in itself, each of them fitting harmoniously into the similar and complementary groups by which it was surrounded, and all of them kept together by the baton of the State-conductor.

The translation of the philosophy into practice, during the eight years from 1926 to 1934, was somewhat topsy-turvy. The corporative idea began to be expressed in law in 1926. It was philosophically defined in Article VI of the Charter of Labour in 1927. It was applied in 1928, in a preliminary and embryonic way, to the composition of the Italian Chamber of Deputies, which was made to depend, in the first instance, on nominations made by national confederations of employers' syndicates and by similar confederations of syndicates of workers. (The effect was that the Chamber became a quasi-corporation, uniting representatives of employers and employed.) The idea was again applied in 1930—but still in a preliminary way—to the composition of a new National Council of Corporations, or economic advisory body, which was made to include (among some other and official elements) representatives designated by the national confederations of employers and of workers, and which thus became, like the Chamber of Deputies, a quasi-corporation. But while the corporative idea was thus applied to the composition both of the Chambers of Deputies and of the National Council of Corporations, it still remained, as it were, in the air. No actual corporation had yet been instituted in any determinate branch of prôduction. It was not until the law of 13 January 1934 had been passed that corporations were actually instituted in the different branches. It was not until May of that year that it was finally announced that twenty-two corporations were to be organised in agriculture, industry, commerce, and the other branches of economic activity.

The idea of the corporative state is thus older than the fact of the corporation. But the corporation itself is the foundation of the whole structure, even though the foundation was the last part of the structure to be built. If we study this foundation, as it appears in the law of 1934 'on the formation and functions of corporations', we find that these corporations ('foreseen', as it is expressed, in the legislation of 1926 and the Charter of 1927) are to be set up by the decree of the Head of the Government, and to act under the presidency of an officer—a Minister, or an Under-Secretary of State, or the Secretary of the Fascist party—appointed by a similar decree. The decree determines the number of members to be designated by each of the syndicates united in any given corporation; and the designation made by each syndicate is to be approved by the Head of the Government. In its composition the corporation is thus a regulated 'organ of the State'; and the same is true of its function. The corporation exercises large powers; but it exercises them under the direction of the State. It can elaborate, for example, rules for the collective regulation of economic relations and the unitarian regulation of production; but it does so on the proposition of the qualified Minister, or at the request of one of the syndicates concerned, with the consent of the Head of the Government. Again, it can draw up tariffs, or rates, for the remuneration of services and for the prices of commodities offered to the public under privileged conditions; but it draws up these rates under the same conditions as those under which it elaborates rules, and the rates become binding only when they are published by the decree of the Head of the Government. In the same way a corporation may give its opinion on questions affecting its branch of economic activity; but it does so at the request of the relevant department of administration. All in all, from beginning to end, the corporation remains, in the terms of the definition which was already enunciated in the decree of 1 July 1926, an 'organ of the administration of the State'.

In a speech which was delivered in the Italian Senate on the day on which the law of 1934 was passed, Signor Mussolini sought to enunciate the fundamental principles of the Fascist corporative economy. It was, he said, an economy of the individual; but it was also an economy of associated groups, and it was also an economy of the State. So far as the individual was concerned, corporative economy was based on respect for private property—provided that it was not merely enjoyed, but used for social purposes: it was based on respect for private enterprise—provided that it was adequate to social necessities. So far as associated groups were concerned, corporative economy was an attempt to introduce order into the economic field by way of the self-discipline of each category. So far as the State was concerned, corporative economy demanded its action in the last resort, as the final arbiter. 'Only...when categories fail to agree and to secure a due balance of forces may the Government intervene. It has the sovereign right to do so, since it represents the other term of the equation—the consumer, the anonymous mass—which being unorganised must be safeguarded by an organ representing the collective body of citizens.' The argument thus stated is lucid; we may even say that it is cogent; but it still leaves room for doubts, or at any rate for questions. There are two questions which seem particularly important. Is the State only the last resort, and does it really permit the associated groups of each category, when once they are united in a corporation, to exercise normally and currently a genuine power of self-discipline? If the corporation of each category is really an organ of the administration of the State—if (in the words already quoted from a resolution presented to the National Council of Corporations in November 1933) it is 'an instrument which, under the *aegis of the State*, *disciplines* the productive forces in view of the wealth, the *political power*, and the well-being of the nation'—we can hardly answer that question in the affirmative. Again (and this is an even more crucial question), are capital and labour evenly balanced and equally married in each corporation? Are the syndicates of workers free associations, able to elaborate their own policies and to throw up their own natural leaders; and can they stand on a level with employers in elaborating rules, drawing up tariffs, giving opinions and performing the other activities of the corporation?

It is perhaps permissible, before facing these questions, to escape into a digression, which may prove to be highly relevant.

On 15 May 1931 (the fortieth anniversary of a famous Encyclical of Leo XIII) the present Pope issued an Encyclical dealing with the fundamental principles of social economics, under the style of *Quadragesimo Anno*. In one passage of the Encyclical he enunciates the general doctrine of corporativism. He argues that a true social system or *ordo* requires for its units not competing individuals or warring classes, but *ordines*, in each of which masters and men co-operate to form one body or 'college' (or, in other words, 'corporation'), and all of which, in their turn, co-operate with one another to promote the common good of the whole society. He adds to this argument a double corollary. First, the *collegium* or *corpus* in which the masters and men of each *ordo* are united must be freely formed (*integrum est hominibus quam maluerint formam eligere*); and secondly, the associations of employers and workers which unite to form it must themselves be voluntary associations, freely instituted and freely choosing the rules and regulations best suited to their end. From this argument, and this double corollary, the Pope turns to a review of 'a peculiar system' which has been instituted along these lines. It is the system (though no country is mentioned by name) of contemporary Italy. In the course of his review the Pope begins by drawing attention to a number of involuntary and coercive elements in the associations, or syndicates, from which the

Italian corporations must necessarily be formed.[1] These elements, it is implied, contravene the second part of the double corollary which has just been stated. The Pope then turns to the corporations themselves—the organs of State (*vera ac propria Status instrumenta*), which are formed from representatives of the syndicates on both sides, and which proceed to direct the syndicates from which they are formed. The advantages which they can produce are obvious—the peaceful association of the activities of different classes: the ending of the doctrine and practice of class-war; the moderating effects of the authority of a special State-organ or 'magistracy'. But there are also dangers. There is the danger that the State, instead of aiding associations, and instead of discharging the ministerial function (*subsidarium officium*) which it owes to them, should substitute itself for their free activity. There is the danger that the new corporative order should smack too much of bureaucracy, and should be used to serve political aims rather than the institution of a better system of social order.

In his speech in the Senate (in January 1934) which has already been quoted Signor Mussolini refers, at any rate by implication, to the danger of bureaucracy. The procedure of the corporations will, he states, be watched. It must be rapid but not bureaucratic—not that some increase of bureaucracy is to be feared, for all human

---

[1] Subscriptions *must* necessarily be paid to the legally recognised syndicates by all the workers or employers in the trade or profession which they cover, and all the workers or employers in a trade or profession *must* conform to any agreement concluded by the legally recognised syndicates covering their trade or profession.

institutions require a measure of bureaucracy. The argument is just; but even if we allow its weight, we are still faced by the fundamental questions which have already been raised, and which are given a new point and edge by the measured words of the papal Encyclical. In particular we have to enquire into the extent of the liberty of association which is left to the syndicates of workers—or in other words, to Trade Unions, in our ordinary English use of that term—under the system of the corporative State. Whatever the corporation itself may be, and whether or no it is bureaucratic, the real issue turns on the nature of its constituent elements, and, above all, on the nature of the constituent element which is furnished by the workers' Trade Unions.

Under the Italian legislation which has been passed since 1926 strikes (and lock-outs) are forbidden; but Trade Unions none the less still continue to exist and act. There are two sorts of Trade Unions of workers. One, which need not be considered, is the unrecognised Trade Union. It may exist; but its action is, in effect, confined to the simple and charitable purpose of a mutual benefit society. The other is the legally recognised Trade Union, which has economic as well as charitable functions, and which alone counts. Legal recognition, and along with it legal personality (or in other words the status of a corporate body, in our English sense of that term), are given to any Trade Union of workers which includes one-tenth of the workers in its branch of industry; but it is a necessary condition of membership that each member should be 'of good moral and political conduct from a national point of view'. The recognised Trade Union is thus necessarily a Fascist union, composed of members who, as Signor Mussolini has said, 'accept the Fascist doctrine and practice', and 'are directed by leaders who are invariably enrolled in the Fascist party'. Only one Trade Union can be legally recognised in any branch of industry; and when once a Trade Union has been recognised in any branch it 'represents legally' all the workers in that branch, whether or no they can satisfy the necessary condition of membership, and whether or no they are actually members. This legal representation involves two consequences or rules. The first is that all the workers in the branch are bound to pay contributions to the legally recognised Trade Union of the branch; the second is that they are all bound and obliged by the collective contracts which it makes. The effect of these rules (which are rules of law) is that the members of the recognised Union, who may be one-tenth of the workers in the trade, control, or at any rate represent, the whole body of workers. But they are themselves, in turn, controlled. In the first place the officials of the Trade Unions are not working-class officials, like the Trade Union officials of our own country. So far as one can discover, in wandering among Italian towns, they come from the professional middle classes; they are, for example, lawyers who, on their way to a practice, may work with a Trade Union in order to acquire experience and connections which will be valuable to them afterwards. In the second place, the officials of the Trade Unions, and indeed the whole working of the Trade Unions, including their current deliberations and their basic *statuti* or articles of association, are subject to the supervision and control of the State. The Minister of

Corporations may annul deliberations: a decree may impose a revision of *statuti*.

Just as, in English law, it is the general rule that whatever is given to or imposed upon a Trade Union of workers shall also be given to or imposed upon a Trade Union of employers (the same name of Trade Union legally covering both sides), so also, in Italian law, the rights and obligations of syndicates of workers are the same as the rights and obligations of syndicates of employers. If there is tutelage, the tutelage, at any rate in law, is equal. But it is pardonable, none the less, to draw particular attention to the status and the disabilities of the workers' syndicates. On that basis it is hard to believe that the corporative system celebrates an equal marriage between the two parties whom it joins. The Trade Unions of workers, with their middle-class officers, can hardly confront the employers and their agents on equal terms. They are not comparable to our own Trade Unions, which are led by their own natural leaders and freely determine their policies in the light of their native tradition. Corporativism is indeed a species of group-philosophy; but it is not a philosophy of group-liberty, and it does not recognise that *libertas consociationes instituendi* which Pius XI proclaims. The working-class groups are depressed groups in comparison with the groups to which they are married. And over them, as over those other groups, there rises the integrating and directing State, welding the groups of both sides together into 'organs of State', and controlling the organs which it creates. Signor Mussolini said truly, in a declaration to the National Council of Corporations in November 1933, that 'for a full, complete and integral corporativism it is necessary to have only one political party and a unitary State'.

So far of corporativism in its relation to the general principle of group-life and group-liberty. But there is also another relation in which it stands. It stands related, and closely related, to the life and liberty of parliament. We have already seen that the corporative idea was applied by a law of 1928 to the composition of the Chamber of Deputies, and by another law of 1930 to the composition of an economic advisory chamber called the National Council of Corporations. By the law of 1928 parties ceased to nominate candidates in territorial constituencies. The whole of Italy became a single constituency; and this constituency voted for a single list of 400 candidates selected by the Grand Council of the Fascist party from a larger preliminary list of 'pre-candidates' nominated, in the main, by national confederations of employers and employed. Instead of political parties with their political principles there were thus substituted economic groups with their economic interests. This in itself was a grave change; and the change is accentuated for us when we note that in the first parliament elected under the law of 1928 the representatives of the confederations of employers preponderated over those of the confederations of the employed. But a graver change was introduced when the new advisory economic chamber was introduced in 1930. This, too, contained representatives designated by the national confederations of employers and employed. In its function, which was a function of advice on economic issues, it differed from the political chamber; but in the principle of its composition it was

7-2

practically a duplicate. Was there room for two bodies which, in the principle of their composition, were merely duplicates? If one of the two had to disappear, must it not be the old Chamber of Deputies, which seemed less immediately and obviously true to the corporative idea, and which in any case was not new-minted and shining? Towards the end of 1933 it seemed as if the old representative chamber of the Italian parliament was sentenced; and speeches began to be made in that sense. Early in 1934, when the law on the formation and functions of corporations was being passed, a reprieve was issued. Signor Mussolini declared that the procedure of the new corporations was to be watched; when sufficient data had been gathered, the time would come for constitutional reform, and the future of the Chamber of Deputies would be decided. The data have now, apparently, been gathered. The Chamber of Deputies is sentenced to extinction. The corporative idea, which requires one political party and a unitary State, requires no parliament—at any rate in the sense in which we use the word 'parliament'.

Whether we think in terms of social economics, or in terms of politics and parliaments, it is hard for us, in this country, to accept the philosophy of corporativism. If we think in the first set of terms, we have to recognise that (at any rate on the workers' side) the associations which are the constituent elements of corporations are not the free economic associations to which we are accustomed; and we have equally to recognise that the corporation itself, which combines the associations from both sides in some given area of the economic field, is neither evenly balanced within nor, as regards its relations to the State without, possessed of genuine powers of 'self-discipline'. Indeed, it is a grave error to speak of the State as standing 'without': the corporation is an organ of the State: the State is within it, and it is within the State. Similarly, if we think in terms of politics and parliaments, we have to recognise that a corporative parliament, based on vocational groups, with all their different interests—based too on a double set of those groups, one for employers and one for workers—is not a homogeneous national parliament such as we know, broad-based on a common will, and expressing great general currents of opinion. But however we may cherish our own institutions, we have no right to make them a general canon. Man may be the measure of all things; but it does not follow that Englishmen are. The unification of our country is an old and established fact; and on the basis of that fact we can permit ourselves a large variety of opinion and a multifarious liberty of action. The unification of Italy is still proceeding. That process of unification (or, in the current phrase, 'totalitarianisation') colours everything. It colours the corporation and all the corporative institutions. But life grows: the process of unification may achieve its alchemy: the intense colour may grow more mellow: the corporative idea may begin to stand out in its own true hues. We may then expect a double development. On the one hand the association, and the corporation of associations, as they begin to find themselves, will tend of themselves towards greater self-discipline and more self-government. On the other hand the State, as it grows more sure of itself and of the cause of unity which it carries, will be ready to treat associations as coadjutors and allies, to whom it owes *subsidarium officium*, and not as 'organs of administration' which owe it a bounden duty of legal obedience.

Yet it may be that these hopes and dreams belong to future years, which many of us will never live to see. Signor Mussolini, in his later speeches, since the beginning of 1936, has laid a new and acuter accent on unification and totalitarianisation.... Not that he has left us entirely without hope of other developments. He asserted vividly, in a speech of the spring of 1936, the equality of the workers, as collaborators in the corporative system, with the owners of capital resources. There is this justification for the assertion, that as things now stand the workers' representatives attend the meetings of the corporations on a footing of nominal equality with the representatives of employers, and may thus gain some insight into the 'unitarian regulation of production'—the one theme hitherto handled by the corporations, for they have not yet dealt with the 'collective regulation of economic relations' between employers and employed. There is thus some hope, if not of partnership, at any rate of education for the workers' representatives in the process of the rationalisation of Italian industry.... But this hope is dashed by another assertion, or proclamation, which was made by Signor Mussolini in the same speech of the spring of 1936. The great industries which work for national defence are, he announced, to be given a 'special character within the orbit of the State', and to be specially subjected to the intervention of the State. When we reflect how much of economic activity may be covered by the idea of 'working for national defence', we cannot but feel that this announcement tends to overshadow and over-cloud any prospect of the development of corporative self-government in Italian industry. All industries of importance for national defence will, according to this policy, be more or less nationalised under a 'regulating plan'. The corporative system may remain in other industries, such as they are; but overshadowed by the other system, and perhaps affected in its own nature by the proximity and the influence of the other system, it may tend to show more and more that it is simply a part of the State and a collection of 'organs of administration'.

It is thus permissible to doubt whether the substitution of the Council of Corporations for the Chamber of Deputies carries Fascist Italy farther forward into a larger air. Certainly the two bodies have seemed to overlap; but the victory of the Council of Corporations also seems to make organs of administration the source and the basis of representative institutions. That is a curious thing. But Signor Mussolini believes and proclaims that when the two changes announced in 1936 are accomplished—the economic transformation and the constitutional innovation—Fascism will have fully realised its fundamental postulates. That is to say, all industry that bears on defence (which may well be all industry) will be specially subjected to the intervention of the State, and parliamentarianism, in our sense, will be gone. Thus, he concludes, the Italian people, thanks to Fascism, sees before it the path to ever-increasing power. Power...that, then, is the end. But is it really the end? Must all things work together for that? Or will the life of the Italian spirit, as it grows, grow in quieter years to mellower fruits? The end is not yet. The new and acuter accent on unification and totalitarianisation is of to-day. To-morrow, and to-morrow, and to-morrow?

VI
PHILOSOPHY AND POLITICS

The Haldane Memorial Lecture, London, 5 June 1934

The question which I have raised, and desire to discuss with you, has a double edge. It suggests two different, and yet connected, issues. Do general philosophies of the world—of space and time, and man's significance in space and time—control or affect the actual politics of States? Is the individual statesman, in his conduct of political affairs, the better, or the worse, for a training in philosophy?

I shall perhaps be illogical, but I shall be human, if I begin by speaking of the latter of these issues. We are all of us interested in the individual and the concrete; and we all of us naturally start our thinking from the particular case. But that is not all. We are assembled here to commemorate the name and the fame of Lord Haldane. He was not only trained in Philosophy: he pursued its study all his days. Not only did he pursue its study: he made it the master-light of all his seeing and doing, both in seasons of calm weather and in that other season, which the vicissitudes of affairs and the veerings of the *popularis aura* may bring to political mariners, when he fell on evil days and tongues. Philosophy to him was a constant and serene star of guidance,

An ever-fixéd mark
That looks on tempests, and is never shaken.

If there was ever a man who carried philosophy into the conduct of affairs, it was he. He made it speak in the Law

Courts, when he argued the case of the United Free Church of Scotland: he made it active in the reform of military administration, and he carried it into the making of a national system of education. What shall we say of his faith?

England is not altogether a pragmatic country. I well remember, some thirty years ago, the building of the great Liberal cabinet which guided the destinies of England without interruption for nearly a decade. When I watched its building, and saw the inclusion of men such as Haldane, and Morley, and Bryce, I said to myself, 'There is still a place for the philosophers'. I had been trained in the *Republic* of Plato; and Plato, you will remember, desired with a great desire that politicians should be philosophers, and philosophers politicians. It happened that I was then writing a work which dealt with Plato; and I recall how I was impelled to remark in a footnote that there was much in modern political conditions that was still reminiscent of Plato, and that a favourite phrase of one of our statesmen (I did not mention his name, but you will readily guess who it was) was the Platonic phrase, 'Put thought into it'. Perhaps I am too much of an optimist; but I am genuinely inclined to think, as I look back over the space of my own lifetime, that thought—philosophic thought—has been put into our politics. Such thought has not been confined to Liberals, though I would confess, in a brief but perhaps provocative parenthesis, that I feel Liberalism to be the natural home of every philosopher. Lord Balfour was also among the philosophers; and I have read works of political philosophy which were written by Mr Ramsay Mac-Donald. (How inevitably these Scottish names recur, when one talks of the concatenation of philosophy with high political office!) But the matter goes beyond individual names; and I would take it to a higher plane. Fundamentally, the influence of philosophy upon politics is the influence of Universities. It is the influence of Oxford and Cambridge, Edinburgh and Göttingen, London and Berlin. The Universities focus philosophic thought, and transmit it to their students; and in every age some of their students, instinct with that thought and carrying it with them into a political career, have transmitted it to their country. I once heard Mr Asquith say, in the hall of New College, Oxford, 'It was in this hall, from the lectures of Alfred Robinson on the *Republic* of Plato, that I learned such lessons of political wisdom as I have since tried to carry into effect.' It was a generous confession, made by a generous soul; and I must not exaggerate its significance. But I cannot refrain, as an old Oxford man, from saying one word about that mingled Oxford course of ancient and modern philosophy and Greek and Roman history which goes by the name of Literæ Humaniores. How many of our statesmen have passed through that course—Peel and Gladstone, Asquith and Morley, Milner and Curzon. I cannot but believe that something of a philosophy of life and politics came to them from that course and from its teachers—teachers such as Mark Pattison and Jowett, T. H. Green and R. L. Nettleship; I cannot but believe that the sovereign lessons of the philosophers, from Plato to Spinoza and from Spinoza to Mill and the critics of Mill, flowed into them, and through them into their fellow-countrymen. Not that Oxford stands alone, or supreme. I cannot forget

Cambridge, or the influence, in my own lifetime, of Henry Sidgwick. I cannot forget London, or the teaching of the early lecturers of University College, under the ægis of Bentham, or the lectures of F. D. Maurice at King's College. It is no one University alone that matters: it is all our Universities together. 'They', as Lord Morley said in an address to the students of Manchester in 1912, 'have been main agents in moulding both our secular and our ecclesiastical politics.' They have still to continue that great work. It may well be that they will continue it with a new distribution of relative importance. Under the old social system it was an aristocratic class, in Universities frequented by that class, which had its day. In our new social system new classes, in new Universities, may be their successors. No matter. The cardinal thing is that philosophy should still be cultivated in Universities, and still be transmitted, by the young men who are strong and enter the battle of politics, into the life of the nation.

I have put one side of the matter, and indeed I have almost given a verdict for it. I have spoken as if philosophers really controlled politics, and as if it were a good thing that they should. But perhaps I am making too much haste. It is true that some men, trained in philosophy, or turning (it may be in later years) to the study of philosophy, have acquitted themselves nobly in political affairs. I have spoken of English examples, but I might also cite in evidence the names of two men, both still living, who belong to other countries. One is the name of Thomas Masaryk, sometime lecturer in comparative Slavonic philology at King's College, now President of Czecho-Slovakia and the maker of a nation, who came to politics by way of a professorship of philosophy and the teaching of Plato's doctrines. The other is that of General Smuts, who has shown the world that it is possible to combine the invention of a new philosophy of 'holism' with legal, political and even military genius. But are there not also examples to the contrary, and may not philosophers in politics be what Matthew Arnold said of Shelley, 'Beautiful but ineffectual angels'? If we count Woodrow Wilson among the philosophers (and at any rate he had a genius for enunciating *principia politica* in statuesque phrases), we may say that he failed to translate his philosophy into effective practice. Sometimes he surrendered principle to the dictates of exigency and the subtleties of more astute politicians; sometimes he stood stiffly on principle to the neglect of accommodation and at the price of practical failure. But this was perhaps the defect of the man rather than the essential nature of the philosophic temper; and in any case we must beware of obeying the precept, *ab uno disce omnes.* Yet it may be said, with some show of evidence, that the philosophic temper readily trends towards what has been called 'the fastidious or pedantocratic school of government'. Plato himself was something of a schoolmaster to bring men perforce to a righteousness which only the elect could see; and Plato was the great prophet of the philosopher-politician. And not only may the philosopher be pedantocratic: he may also be purblind. He may not have a quick tact for the nuances of human feelings and the inner sap of human affairs. He may see men as shadows, walking dimly, but not as real creatures of flesh and blood: he may see the things which are above, but not the things which are tumbling at his feet. Masaryk himself, philosopher and Platonist, has protested against what he calls 'school-master politics'—the spirit of the dogmatists and doctrinaires who 'tend too frequently to be absolutist, self-willed, cranky and childish when they become members of parliament and ministers, or attain public office and dignity'. He has confessed, too, that 'the academically educated...is often inferior to the experienced organiser and party-leader in knowledge of men and in practical capacity for dealing with parties, parliament and government'. In a somewhat similar sense we find Lord Morley, whom no man would ever accuse of disrespect for philosophy or philosophers, laying stress on 'the intuitive instinct that often goes farther in the statesman's mind than deliberate analysis or argument'. He cites in evidence a saying of Bismarck, when he was once reminded that he used to sit at dinner with the philosopher Schopenhauer, and that Schopenhauer had preached the priority of self-conscious thought to the action of the will. 'I daresay that may be all right; for myself, at least, I have often noticed that my will had decided before my thinking was finished.'

Here is a formidable list of qualities in which the philosopher-politician may be alleged to be deficient. One of these we may call by the name of tact and knowledge of men. A second is intuitive instinct. A third is rapidity of decision. They are connected; and perhaps we may take the middle term of the three—intuitive instinct—as broad enough to imply and involve the general indictment of the philosopher-politician. Is politics essentially a matter of intuitive instinct, arising from tact and knowledge of men and issuing in instant decision, or is it a matter, in the last resort, of some philosophic view of time and space and man? It is a question as old as the *Meno* of Plato. Here Plato pits intuitive instinct—or, as he calls it ὀρθὴ δόξα, the gift of the happy guess—against the true understanding which has to be got by philosophic study. Intuitive instinct, he admits, may carry a man very far. It is in politics what divination is in religion; and the intuitive statesman, 'having no understanding, but being inspired and possessed', may say and do much that is noble. Such statesmen are known to history: indeed we have had a brilliant example in our own time. They do not satisfy Plato. They cannot, he feels, transmit their gift of the happy guess, or make it a permanent tradition of politics; and what is more, they may fail to guess right at a crucial moment, and gravely mislead the state. Plato accordingly gives his verdict for the statesman who is grounded on an understanding of principle—the man who can teach and transmit what he knows; the man who has his own secure anchorage in any gust of emergency, and can ride out any storm of trouble,

> Or if an unexpected call succeed,
> Come when it will, is equal to the need.

We may add some further reflections to those suggested by Plato. For one thing, intuitive instinct is generally concerned with means and manœuvres: it does not apprehend, nor is it calculated to apprehend, the sovereign ends and the final purposes which lie beyond means and manœuvres. For another thing, those immediate decisions which seem to proceed in a flash from instinct and to anticipate conscious thinking have often a more remote and more glorious ancestry. We may not be conscious of thought at the moment; but there has generally been a long process of incubation, in the mind of any true statesman, which is the true explanation and cause of what may seem sudden decisions. Bismarck was perhaps a better philosopher than he knew.

But we shall not settle our problem of the relation of philosophy to politics if we stay at the level of an enquiry into individual statesmen, and if we limit ourselves to asking whether they are or should be philosophers, of the conscious or unconscious variety. We must turn to the larger question, which has already been mentioned, and was only postponed because it confronted us with a vast and general impersonality—the question whether philosophies of human life are the great forces which affect or control the actual politics of states. If we answer that question in the affirmative—if we say, with Hegel, that ideas have hands and feet, and their hands may grasp us, and their feet run forward swiftly with us in their grasp— if we admit that the actual politics of many of our modern states are simply actualised and realised philosophies— then the lesser of our questions receives a ready answer. A statesman must necessarily be a philosopher when the State in which he lives is an actualised philosophy. He must be competent either to apprehend and to apply the dominant philosophy, or to construct and to apply the corrective of a counter-philosophy. There is no third choice.

It may be said that all revolutions are philosophies, or at any rate based on philosophies. These great upheavals of the human mind, which issue in new and revolutionary

States, proceed from profound depths in the thought of man. I believe that to be true of our English Revolution of 1688: I believe it, still more certainly, to be true of the French Revolution of 1789: I believe it, most certainly of all, to be true of the Russian Revolution of 1917. Let me linger, for a moment, over the Russian Revolution and the Russian revolutionary State. I have spoken of more than one philosopher in politics: I have not yet spoken of the one who seems to me, in many ways, the greatest of them all—not in the truth of his philosophy, and not in the method of its application, but in its terrible intensity and the fiery dynamic of its translation. That philosopher was Lenin. I do not say that his philosophy was original. It never professed to be. The philosophy of Lenin, in his own conception, was the consummation, by a natural process of evolution, of the philosophy of Marx and Engels, as their philosophy, in its turn, was the consummation, by the same process, of all previous philosophies from Spinoza down to Hegel. There was a work published, about a year ago, by Dr Julius Hecker, which bears the title, *Moscow Dialogues: Discussions on Red Philosophy*. I think I had already realised, when I read Lenin's own pamphlet on *The State and Revolution*, that I was face to face with a genuine philosophy, even if it was a philosophy with which I could not agree. I realised it more deeply, far more deeply, when I read Dr Hecker's work. Let me quote two sentences. 'We are proud to trace our origin', so Dr Hecker makes the communist Socrates of his dialogues say, 'not only to Kant, Fichte and Hegel, but to the English and French materialists, and through them to the greatest mind of modern philosophy, Baruch Spinoza.

All these have been synthetically and materialistically re-valuated in the work of Marx, Engels and Lenin.' I do not think that these are idle words—not for a moment. I believe that the man who made the Russian Revolution had attained a philosophy, and was actualising a philosophy—actualising it as by fire. The old Greek philosophers were not content to leave a philosophy as a mere philosophy. They wanted to make it also a way of life—a way of life for a community of men. The same is true of the new Russian philosophers. They have found a philosophy, and made it a way of life for a whole community. We shall not understand Russian politics to-day unless we realise that they are a concrete philosophy of this order. That is why there is passion behind them, and a sort of religious fire. That is why they cannot be met, upon their own ground, except by some sort of counter-philosophy.

I might pass from Russia to China, which in the more recent phases of its revolution has been affected by Russia. I might speak of Sun Yat Sen, and his book called *San Min Chu I*, with its philosophy half of communism, half of nationalism, which has become the gospel of Chinese politics and been made the basis of Chinese education. But I prefer to turn to Central Europe; for here, in Germany and in Italy, we have seen revolutions, and we have been confronted by philosophies, which touch our own life more nearly. Italy, under the guidance of Fascism, has developed an old philosophy—the philosophy of Nationalism—to a new pitch of intensity. The core of Fascism is a belief in the transcendency of the meta-physical Nation, conceived as an organism which has a being, and ends and means of action, superior to those of its members. This belief issues in a totalitarian conception of the government of the State, as controlling wholly the life of all its members by virtue of being the guardian of the metaphysical Nation: it issues again in a corporative conception of the handling of economics, through groups of employers and workers acting together under the ægis of the government in the interest of national welfare. This is the philosophy incarnate in the Fascist party, expounded in the Italian press and Italian literature, and taught in the Italian Universities—a philosophy actualised not only in politics, but also in every manifestation of social life. The new Germany of National Socialism has built itself upon a parallel, and yet different, philosophy. The core of its belief is not the metaphysical Nation, but the physical Race—the physical Race of the Aryan type, conceived as the appointed treasury of pure culture and true progress. This is a belief which issues in emphasis on physical heredity and the importance of stock and breed. Its goal is a brave new world constructed on the eugenic basis of the best of the Aryan stock. Totalitarianism is its consequence, because such a new world will only come by scientific direction. Here again a philosophy, drawn to political consequences and actualised in politics, has enthroned itself in the chair of government. Whether we look at Moscow or Nanking, Berlin or Rome, we must admit that ideas have hands and feet—grasping hands and hurrying feet.

It is the danger of philosophies when they actualise themselves in politics that they become philosophies of compulsory conformity. When philosophy is only a matter of philosophic schools, we shall see rival schools and a healthy competition of their conflicting tenets. When a single philosophy climbs the throne, and clutches the crown, men put their necks under a tyranny of conformity. Perhaps any philosophy tends to this consequence; but the tendency is accentuated when a philosophy is based not on the conception of the intrinsic value of the individual human personality, but on a conception of the sanctity and the supremacy of the group. All the three philosophies of which I have spoken—the Communist, the Fascist, the National Socialist—may be said to have sprung from group feeling; and they actively glorify and intensify that from which they have sprung. For the Communist, the group which he calls the proletariat has its sanctity; for the Fascist, the organism of the nation, transcending all its members, has the supremacy; for the National Socialist, the Aryan race has a primacy, and the glory of blood, and of the State based on blood, is no shadow, but the one substantial thing. We are face to face with the insurrection of Titanic groups, which have taken to themselves their different forms of group-philosophy, and are hurling them, as the Titans hurled rocks at Olympus, through our European world.

What is to be done? Our argument, which was intended to vindicate a place for philosophy in the conduct of politics, seems to have twisted in our hands. Philosophy, it would now appear, not only possesses a place: it possesses too much of a place, and is the peril of our times. From this we might hastily conclude that the cure of our present disorders would be to banish philosophy and philosophers from our States (as Plato wished to banish poetry and poets from his), and to cultivate common sense. Such a conclusion would not only be hasty: it would also be very unwise. When philosophy is troubling our political world so sorely, the right course is not to abrogate it, but to cultivate it more. It is an old saying that there would be no need of metaphysics and philosophy if it were not that bad metaphysics and wrong philosophy existed, and had to be refuted. For myself, I should say that some reflection about

The ends of being and ideal grace

was always necessary; but I should hasten to add that it was especially necessary in this turbulent and fascinating age of heaving and seething nations and their conflicting philosophies. It is good to be alive in these days. But these are also days in which all who can think have a special duty to put thought into their work, and to contribute what they can to the common stock of the thought of the world. It is a duty particularly incumbent upon the young men and women of our Universities, and upon their teachers; it is a duty very particularly, and very gravely, incumbent upon all who have set themselves, in public office and in all places of social authority, to be leaders of the people by their counsels, and by their knowledge of learning meet for the people.

What is happening to us to-day? I should say, in a phrase which may be obscure, but which I will endeavour to explain, that what is happening is the attainment of a new self-consciousness of their existence by the peoples of the world, and, with that, the rise of questionings about the purposes of their existence and the methods of their existence. For centuries our human societies have acquiesced in the government of some élite, generally an élite of birth, which has been content to guide their destinies along traditional lines of social order and foreign policy. We have now gone into the melting-pot, and we cannot but think about the process. Great economic changes, accompanied by a propaganda of new doctrines of social life and economic structure: the spread of new systems of national education: the disturbances of great wars—these forces, and many more, have impinged on every constituted society, and plunged it into self-questioning. What is the thing called a people—be it in Russia or Germany or Italy? What is the point of its existence, and what is it here, in this world, to do? What is the relation of its members to its existence and its doing? Have they come into the world to laud and magnify its name—to work for some economic plan which is the point of its being, or to be cells in its organic unity, or to be drops of pure blood in its racial purity? Or have they come into the world as living souls, in order to be and to realise themselves, all working in mutual help and charity, but each, none the less, an end in himself?

We are driven back upon ultimate questions, and we can only face them frankly. I do not think I exaggerate when I say that they are upon us, or when I talk about a new self-consciousness of existence among the peoples of the world, and a new questioning about the purposes of their existence. We have only to look at the world around us. At one end, China is conning the philosophy of Sun Yat Sen: at another end Washington, under the guidance of Mr Roosevelt, is wondering whether there is not more wisdom to be found than is written in the Declaration of Independence and the constitution of the United States.

In and between there is a battle of schools of social philosophy. Communism and Fascism, Socialism and Syndicalism, Conservatism and Liberalism, Nationalism and Internationalism—their name is legion. The fates are upon us. Therefore, in those words of Homer which one of our statesmen, Lord Carteret, loved, 'since they are upon us, and no man may escape or avoid them, let us go forward...'. But in what direction? There are two things which I should like to say in answer.

First, we must, to the best of our ability, let the various philosophies compete freely in our midst. We must practise the high virtue of philosophic tolerance. We must not enthrone a single philosophy by compulsion, or stop the great debate of different theories which is the essence of philosophic method. There are indeed some limits which must be set to freedom of the expression of thought. They are being discussed in England to-day, under the head of incitement to disaffection. I would set the limits as far back as I could, remembering that Communism is not a disease, but an honest if extreme doctrine which has to be debated and discussed. I would always say to myself, 'Let every philosophy come into the debate, and show whether it has enough power—which means whether it has enough truth—to survive.' There is a corollary to this saying. If variety of doctrines is to survive, variety of parties must also survive. Parties are the social forces which precipitate and form doctrines, and translate them into programmes of policy. Doctrines without parties are anæmic: parties without doctrine are commercial companies for the acquisition of office and patronage. We must not enthrone a single party, or make our ideal the institution of a single party State. Upon this, in turn, there is a still further corollary to be drawn. If it be good that variety of doctrine should survive, and if it be good that variety of party should survive, it is good that democracy should survive. The essence of democracy is not voting, or decision by mathematical majorities. It is debate and discussion, and decision by the weight of argument. There can be no democracy unless there are different doctrines, and different parties to discuss the different doctrines. Here I would add a further reflection —or, if you will, a paradox. I have said that the method of democracy is the method of debate; and I have said, or implied, that the method of philosophy is the same. Does it not follow that the method of democracy is the true philosophic method, and that the true philosopher, far from being fastidious or pedantocratic, will be a democrat? Plato said that it was impossible for a whole people to be philosophic. It may also be said, in the opposite sense, that the only thing which can be philosophic, in matters of government, is the whole people. If you can get a whole people to debate, and to decide issues by the weight of argument—if you can achieve, as Milton dreamed, 'a nation subtle and sinewy to discourse'—you have reached the height of government, and realised the philosopher's ideal. But that height will not be reached, or that ideal achieved, in a moment. We have an electorate of 30,000,000. What a work is set before the thinker and teacher—to penetrate and imbue this electorate with thought. What a field is here for adult education, which can serve to cultivate this electorate to the height of its power and its potentiality. Was not Lord Haldane wise, when he set the hopes of his maturest years on the scope and the promise of such education? I come to my second point. Let us suppose that we have a whole people, conscious of its existence and concerned about the purposes of its existence—a people democratically organised, with different parties presenting their different philosophies to its choice—a people ready to discuss the alternatives, and to choose according to the weight of argument. That is much; but it is not all. We have still to face the problem of guidance—the problem of finding the truly trained statesman who can guide the choice, and give it effect when it has been finally made. Every society, however educated it may be, needs some élite for its guidance. In that sense aristocracy has always to be added to democracy, if we take aristocracy in its true sense of the government of the best. The problem is to discover the best. This was the problem which occupied Plato, and which he sought to solve by a system of philosophic training backed by tests and trials. In England to-day we face the problem in a way which is half Platonic and half empiric. We are Platonic in that we have now a ladder of education, and a system of examination at each rung of the ladder, which selects the best capacity from the general community and encourages it to emerge. We are empiric in that, so far as politics are concerned, we leave it to those who have the bent to find a constituency; to out-argue the other candidate, or at any rate to get him out-voted; and then to prove in parliamentary debates, if they get the chance, that they are worthy of being considered for a place in a Ministry. Perhaps there is some sense in our empiricism: at any rate men have to debate their way into leadership, and that is no bad qualification in a system of government which goes on the basis of debate. Meanwhile there has suddenly swung into view, under the general name and style of Fascism, another method. I shall call it the method of natural emergence. A leader emerges, whom 'the people recognises by his marks', as the Tibetans do their grand Lama; but the marks in this case are not physical—they are the marks, as it is expressed in the preamble to the *statuto* of the Italian Fascist Party, 'of his will, his force, and his work'. We all know the leaders in Germany and Italy: in England—I name no name. Once emerged, the leader freely chooses the best of his followers for his assistants, on the basis of past loyalty mixed with future promise: if he is wise, it is said, he also dismisses them freely. Well, there have often been 'Chieftains'; and loyalty to the Chieftain has often been a passport to office. The new continental doctrine of leadership is very old.

I am inclined to think that there is much to be said for our English method of discovering the best, with its mixture of what I have called empiric and Platonic characteristics. Some have quarrelled with the empiric side of our method, which plunges men into the hurly-burly of contested elections and the quagmires of parliamentary procedure: they have said that it does not elicit the best, who may be too shy or too disdainful to face such experiences. I have heard it suggested that the electorate should not vote for persons, but only for programmes; and that a small and wise college of selection should then choose at its discretion, in the light of its knowledge of men and affairs, the men whom it knew to be really fitted to represent and execute programmes, assigning to each programme a number of such men proportionate to the number of votes which had been given in its favour. I doubt if such a method would give us a better or a more philosophic élite. In a system of democratic government based on the process of debate the leaders should properly emerge by showing their powers of debate, and a college of selection which ousted the electorate from the selection of persons, and stopped the possibility of living contact between the electorate and the member of its choice, might not only fail to get better men, but would purchase a new and dubious aristocracy at the price of surrendering the greater part of democracy. If we would improve ourselves, it is the Platonic side of our methods, rather than the empiric, which we should be wise to consider. In other words we must turn our attention to that preliminary selection of the best, and that preliminary training of the best for the high career of politics, which can be achieved in our places of education, and particularly in our Universities. Not—I hasten to add—that University-trained men will ever be, or ever should be, the whole of our parliament and government. Far from it. There will always be many who are drawn directly from the Trade Unions and the ranks of the workers—men who have established themselves by their speech and action in the confidence of their fellows: men who have the feel of life, the experience of life, and the shrewd philosophy of life, which belongs to those who maintain the state of the world by the work of their craft. There will also be those who are drawn directly from the conduct of great businesses and industries—men, it may be, never trained in Universities, but versed in large undertakings, and ready to bring their experience to the business of the State. None the less, if our national system of education, and its apex the University, does its duty of discovering and furnishing to the community the best capacity, there must always be in politics a body of men who have been selected by the process of education and trained for their calling in our Universities. What is the nature of the training which the University should be prepared to give to those who may afterwards serve the State in the guidance of its affairs? The answer which, so far as I know, is generally given on the Continent to-day is that it should be a training in law and economics. I would not decry such studies; but I cannot feel that they are enough. Law and economics are static studies; they may include some historical element, but they deal in the main with the *status quo*. They are again, in the main, studies of means and methods: they do not lead immediately, though they must always ultimately lead, to questions of ends and final purposes. The course which I should desire to see established in all our Universities, for the training of those who may one day serve the State, is a course which combines some study of history and the evolution of man with a study of philosophy and the significance of human life in time and space. I confess that I speak as an old Oxford man, still subject to the 'idols' and the prejudices of my old University. But I cannot but admire two of the Oxford courses I have known—the old course which I have mentioned, dating back to 1800, and combining ancient history with philosophy: the new course which was instituted somewhere about 1920, and which combines modern history and philosophy, along with some study, in their light, of politics and economics, in order that the student may attain some understanding, as the regulations for the course express it, 'of the structure and of the philosophical, political and economic principles of modern society'.

It is a hard thing to get such understanding of principles; and for myself I can only say, as I near the end of a lifetime, that I see them now a little more clearly than I once did. But you young students of to-day start farther on than I did, forty years ago; and you will go farther. There is urgent need that you should. I can only reiterate, as I end, what I have tried to suggest in the course of my address. These are days of the self-consciousness of the peoples of the earth, and of the raising of ultimate questions about the purposes of their existence. They are days of clamant philosophies, actualising themselves in politics—Communism, Fascism of this and that variety, Racialism. You have to study: you have to judge: you have to choose: you have to serve—and it may be to guide—your country, according to your choice. Will you choose, for example, Racialism, and be a follower of what some are beginning to call 'the English mystery'—the mystery or mastery of the English blood; and you will pin your faith to the coming race of eugenic Englishmen? Or will you choose to be that sort of Englishman who, without shedding his Englishry, can also be a citizen of the world; and will you pin your faith not on the purification of some particular blood-stream, but on the education of the common human spirit to an understanding of its common human purposes? The choice is before you—and other choices too. Let me quote, as I end, some words from Plato. 'Mortal souls, behold a new cycle of life and mortality. Your genius will not be allotted to you, but you will choose your genius. The responsibility is with the chooser.'

VII
FOUNDATIONS OF
POLITICS

The Fison Memorial Lecture, London, 19 June 1935

A State is a community of men living under a scheme of law which is backed, in the last resort, by the application of force. What is this community trying to do when it promulgates law and proceeds to enforce the law which it promulgates? It is obviously trying, by collective effort, to better the lives of its members. At the best, it will seek to better the lives of all its members. At the worst, it will seek to better the lives of some. Let us take it at its best, and assume that it is trying to better the lives of all. What is the nature of the betterment? In what respect, or respects, does a political community seek to produce, by the agency of law, a better life among all its members?

There are various answers which may be given to this question. There are some who are votaries of what we may call 'the State biological'. Their concern is for the human body; and they desire the State to act for its betterment. They regard man as a physical organism, engaged in the world of physical nature: they regard a community of men as a sort of natural species, composed of a number of similar organisms: they want each man, and the whole community, to be physically sound and physically true to the particular type of the species. The aim is fit specimens and a pure species, free from whatever is diseased or hybrid: the means are partly the means of preventive and curative medicine, and partly the more positive means, dear to many biologists and to some anthropologists, of eugenic breeding and racial selection. That is one sort of view of human betterment, and that is one sort of conception—a conception perhaps best exemplified in contemporary Germany—of the foundations of politics. Then, in the second place, there are those who regard man as essentially a wealth-producing animal. They, too, are concerned with the physical and material, but the matter with which they are concerned is not the physique and the physical qualities of the human body: it is the matter which is used in the process of economic production; it is the material methods—the machines, the forms of labour and the general technique—which are applied to the process. Those who adopt this point of view are votaries of the State economic. They desire the form of State which is most efficient in the production and the dissemination of wealth; they identify human betterment with the betterment of these economic processes. Next, and not far removed from these votaries of the State economic, there are those who may be called the votaries of the utilitarian State. For them the foundations of politics are not biological or economic: they are rather what we may call by the name of psychological. The utilitarian regards man not as a physical organism or a wealth-producing animal, but rather as a nervous system, or a centre of psychical sensation, equipped with acute and sensitive tentacles which move eagerly towards pleasure and draw back anxiously from pain. If pleasure be identified with the enjoyment of wealth, and pain with the suffering of poverty—and the identification is one which can readily be made—this third school may easily pass into the second, and the second, again, may easily turn into the third. Whatever may be its particular form, the utilitarian State will have for its end the general diffusion of satisfaction—the maximisation of pleasure, the minimisation of pain, the increase of general pleasure, the decrease of general pain. Much will depend upon the ideas which are held by the votaries of the utilitarian State in regard to the nature of the social unit which is to be satisfied by being furnished with pleasure and by being guarded from pain. We should naturally expect that unit to be the individual, who after all is the obvious centre of psychical sensation. If our expectation is fulfilled, as it was in the theory of the Benthamites, the foundation of politics will be individualistic utilitarianism. But it is possible to hold the view that the unit which ought to be satisfied is the social class—either one particular class which is held to be in particular need of satisfaction, or all classes simultaneously, so far as all, with their different needs and wants, can be simultaneously satisfied. On this basis the foundation of politics will be social utilitarianism. It will be the aim of the State to satisfy social wants which are felt by whole social groups.

There is still another view of the nature of human betterment and the purpose of the State. This is the view which is held by the votaries of the State ethical—the State which is based not on biological, nor economic, nor psychological, but on moral foundations. 'True politics', Kant once said, 'cannot take a single step forward unless it has first done homage to morals.'[1] On this basis the primary fact about man, and the fact which constitutes

[1] *Perpetual Peace*, Appendix I, *ad finem*. I owe the quotation, and much else, to Mr E. F. Carritt's book on the relations of morals and politics.

the ultimate foundation of any political community, is the fact that he is a moral being. As such a being he feels and acknowledges moral obligation: in other words, he knows and recognises that other beings, of the same nature as himself, have claims upon him—claims to be treated as free; claims to be treated as equal; claims to be treated justly, by a due keeping of promises made and a due reward for work done—and he equally knows and recognises, by the same token, that he has a responsibility to them for meeting the claims they have upon him. Moral claims, and their answering moral responsibilities—these are the foundations of politics. The better life which the State seeks to produce among its members by the agency of law is a better moral life. It seeks to aid them—only to *aid* them, for the responsibility is fundamentally and essentially their own individual responsibility—to meet the claims which are made upon them, as moral beings, by other similar beings; and the way in which it seeks to aid them is by putting its agency of law, and the force which stands behind the agency of law, at the service of moral obligation. When that is done, and in the area in which it is done, I shall find myself legally obliged, under the constraint of a law backed by force, to treat my fellows on the principles to which I am already morally obliged—to treat them as equal; to treat them as free; to treat them justly, duly keeping my promises to them and duly rewarding their services to me. Not that the legal obligation supersedes the moral obligation. It is a reinforcement, and not a supersession. Moral obligation always remains —the permanent rock; the abiding foundation. And if there be a law which is not built on this foundation—a law which contravenes, instead of aiding, my moral obligation—well, it will be a law, and there will be legal obligation; but I shall be morally obliged to act as if there were no such law, and to disobey the law in the name of the foundation of the law. The moral foundations of politics, in the last resort, are superior to politics. There have always been martyrs to this truth, from the days of Socrates to the days of Sir Thomas More, and even to our own troubled days. Indeed there will always be martyrs to it, so long as law is made by fallible men who are liable to forget the rock of its foundation.

You will see, from what I have said, that I have a belief in the State's *one* foundation—the foundation of moral duty. But I would not for an instant press the idea of the one foundation to an extremity of logic. Man is a composite being. If he is supremely a moral being, he is also, after all, a physical organism, and a wealth-producing animal, and a centre of psychical sensations. There is a sense in which we may say that there is more than one foundation of politics. If the foundation of moral duty is the ultimate rock, there are also other foundations which are biological, and economic, and psychological. They, too, have their appointed place, and I wish to discuss their place. I wish to suggest that it is not separate, or independent. I wish to argue that whenever we talk in terms of these other foundations, we are driven back, sooner or later, on moral considerations. Man is indeed a composite being, but his final and ultimate sovereign is moral obligation; and whatever compartment of his life we investigate, we shall find that it ultimately raises moral problems, which must be solved by moral principles.

Let us try to discuss, from this point of view, the physical, or medical, or biological, foundation of politics. We should all agree, without a moment's demur, that one of the indubitable elements in the composition of man is his body. We should all instinctively assume that one of the indubitable duties of individuals, and equally of communities of individuals, is to preserve and improve the health of the body. On the basis of that instinctive assumption we may well marvel—for indeed it is, at first sight, a very astonishing thing—that it should have taken States so many centuries to realise their simple medical function; to recognise the physical foundation of politics; to acknowledge that a better physical stock is the necessary basis of a better community. In our own country any legislation specifically directed to public health is almost a matter of my own lifetime: at any rate it is safe to say that if public health acts started in 1848 there was no real sanitary code before the Act of 1875. It is true that after we had once begun to move we moved with a great celerity. We have travelled far in the last two generations. The health of the child has been made one of the pillars of our system of public education. The Housing of the Working Classes Act, passed in 1890, was the precursor of a series of Acts intended to secure healthy homes for the labouring population. Before the War there had just been established a scheme of health insurance designed to provide medical care and attendance for the mass of the nation. But in spite of this progress it may fairly be said, without any cynicism, that it needed war and the shock of death to make us fully alive to the problems of peace and the needs of life. It was war that taught us the difference between A1 and C3. We realised that we needed health when it came to confronting death. The physical foundations of politics were only bared and revealed by the wash and the deluge of war.

War is indeed, as an ancient Greek writer said, 'a violent teacher', but the lesson of the duty of the State to the cause of public health is anterior to war, superior to war, and independent of war. It is a duty which arises, like all the political duties of the State, from the fundamental fact of moral obligation. Every human being, I should argue, has a moral claim to the enjoyment of the conditions of physical health. He has this claim at all times, whether in war or in peace. Corresponding to this moral claim, there is an answering moral obligation; and each of us is therefore morally bound to satisfy this claim, wherever we feel that we are personally involved (in our household, for instance, or in our neighbourhood), and to do so by providing, so far as we can, the conditions claimed from us. It is a simple matter of my duty to my neighbour; and I acknowledge this duty, and the right which is the other side of the duty, whenever I subscribe to a voluntary hospital—I try to satisfy, because I feel that I ought to satisfy, a claim of my neighbour upon me. The question then arises, 'who is my neighbour?' In a political community, or State, we are bound to answer that every member of the community, every citizen, is our neighbour. Every member has a claim on every other; every member has a responsibility to every other. The Government of the community is the clearing-house of these claims and responsibilities. This does not mean that it takes them all over, and turns every moral claim into a legal right and every moral responsibility into a legal duty. Far from it...very far from it. It only means that the Government selects some claims—those which have an elementary strength, such as the claim to the enjoyment of the conditions of physical health—and proceeds to turn the responsibility for meeting these claims into a legal duty, in *some* respects, and to *some* extent, but not wholly and entirely. It is now my legal duty, for example, to contribute a quota for the insurance of the health of my servants and employees. It is also my legal duty to contribute my share to the taxes of the State, from which a further quota is contributed by the State in aid of the insurance of all that great majority of my fellow-citizens who are legally insurable. In these respects, and to this extent, my moral responsibility has been turned into a legal duty. But in other respects, and in the general area which is not covered by legislation, my moral responsibility still remains. I have still a moral duty to the cause of the health of my neighbours. I am still bound, by my own conscience, to contribute to the cause of voluntary hospitals. I am still bound, by my own conscience, to visit and relieve the sick. All that the State has done has been to make *some* part of the responsibility for meeting *some* of the claims upon me into a matter of legal duty. For that part, and in respect of those claims, it has built a legal structure. But it has built that structure on the moral foundation—the foundation of moral claims and moral responsibility—which is always the ultimate foundation of politics. And whatever has been built upon it, the foundation still remains, and remains as the immediate basis of the greater part of our lives. It is not what the

State legally bids us do, but what our own conscience morally commands us to do, which controls the greater part of our action.

I have been trying to deal, in these observations, with what I may call the philosophy of public health legislation, so far as such legislation has been attempted hitherto by the English State. But legislation may be attempted, and has been attempted by other States, which carries a concern for physical health, or for the physical quality of the body politic, to further reaches and larger consequences. There is such a thing as eugenic legislation. There is such a thing as racial legislation. What are the ultimate foundations of legislation of this character?

Eugenic legislation, at the first blush, seems to be based specifically and purely on biological foundations. Its aim is the biological aim of selection for survival of the fittest elements. The methods of such selection, when it is applied in a human community, and applied by the Government of that community, will usually be negative. The Government will not select the fit elements, and then use positive measures to encourage their reproduction. It will select the unfit elements, and it will seek, by negative measures, to prevent their reproduction. A recent German law, which came into effect on New Year's Day 1934, may serve to illustrate this policy. It is entitled, 'a law for the prevention of offspring suffering from hereditary disease'. It provides for the compulsory sterilisation of persons who are afflicted with transmissible defects—permanent insanity, congenital epilepsy, hereditary blindness and deafness, congenital physical deformities.

Such legislation may seem to be like the system of

public health legislation with which we are already familiar in England. Superficially it has some likeness; but it is fundamentally different. It is one thing that the State should take heed to the bodies of its members by providing a framework of public health in which each one of us, accepted as a given fact of existence in his own individual right, can make the best of himself: it is another thing, and a very different thing, that the State should take heed to the bodies of its members by a method of selective discrimination. Unlike the true physician, concerned with genuine medicine, who accepts the fact of our existence, and seeks to give us all a greater vitality which brings a larger liberty, the eugenic legislator is critical of the right of individual existence, selective of human material, inimical to some of its elements, preferential in his treatment of others. He is, in the biblical sense of the word, 'a respecter of persons'. He may plead that he is true to nature; that he is building upon her biological foundations: that he is imitating her process of natural selection. But the very fact that he is imitating nature means that he is something different from nature, just as the artist who paints a landscape is different from what he seeks to paint. An imitation of natural selection is not the same as natural selection. It is something consciously created. It is, in that sense, *artificial* selection. It is a deliberate act of discrimination, done by human beings among human beings. As such it has to be judged, in the last resort, by the moral principles which govern such acts. Once more we are driven back on the moral foundations of politics.

Can eugenic legislation be justified by reference to these

foundations? It is possible to argue that I have a claim upon certain persons, suffering from certain defects, that they shall not breed children, because, if they do so, their children will be defective, and that will involve their making claims for assistance on me, or on my children, which we cannot be expected to meet, or which we can only meet at the cost of neglecting other and stronger claims upon us. If we argue in that way, we may come to the conclusion that the State ought to turn our claims upon such persons that they should refrain from breeding children into a legal right that they should be forcibly prevented from breeding by appropriate legislation. I cannot but feel that if the argument is put in that way—and I see no other way in which it can be properly put, when we get down to fundamentals—it may make us a little uneasy. Many of us would find it difficult to say that we had a claim, which the State ought to turn into a right, to have X and Y and Z sterilised. We should find it easier to say that X and Y and Z had a claim upon us for such medical attention, and such medical advice, that they could either breed children in safety or learn for themselves that they had better not breed any children, but submit to voluntary sterilisation. In any case it is always necessary to remember that X and Y and Z are human beings, who are also entitled, as such, to make some simple and fundamental claims. One of these claims is the claim to be treated as free—unless, for some greater cause, which has to be very great indeed, freedom may be properly taken away. Another is the claim to be treated as equal—unless for some greater cause, which has to be very great indeed, equality, too, may be properly taken away. We have to take *all* claims into consideration, and to weigh them *all* against one another, before we are entitled to invoke the State to put its agency of law at the service of any particular claim. I am not arguing that the State may not rightly pass eugenic legislation, and even go to the length of providing for compulsory sterilisation. I am only arguing that, before it does so, it must get down to the moral foundations of politics. The State cannot enforce a rule of artificial selection because the scientist has discovered a principle of natural selection. It can only enforce a rule which confers rights and imposes duties on human beings when it is sure that some moral claim and some answering moral responsibility is so strong, and so much deserving of support, that it may safely be made a matter of legal right and duty.

A new phenomenon of our time is racial legislation. This, too, is selective and discriminatory—not on the ground of physical defect, and not with the consequence of preventing reproduction of the species by those who are physically unfit, but on the ground of physical type, or blood, or stock, and with the consequence of preventing the enjoyment of full civic rights by those who are defective on that ground. Racial legislation and eugenic legislation run readily into one another, as they are doing in Germany to-day; but they are none the less two different things. The canon of racial legislation is not that the unfit shall be discouraged or debarred from producing children: it is rather that alien and uncongenial blood shall not be allowed to mix with some given racial blood-stream, and that the contamination of that blood-stream shall be prevented, first by the attaching of civic disabilities and a consequent social inferiority to persons of alien blood, and secondly by the attaching of similar disabilities and a similar inferiority to persons who, though themselves of pure blood, have mixed their blood with that of the alien. If we enquire into the reasons on which this canon is based, we find that they are not really physical, or at any rate not purely physical. A given blood is selected for favour, and another blood is subjected to discrimination, not because of itself, or in virtue of its own physical quality, but because of the *ideas* which it carries, or is supposed to carry, and in virtue of the quality of the *culture* with which it is connected, or supposed to be connected. One blood-stream is held to be good, because it necessarily and inherently carries an argosy of good ideas; another is held to be bad because it carries, with the same inevitability, a freight of bad ideas. In the last resort, a policy of racial legislation is a policy of discrimination against ideas. It involves a deliberate act of discrimination, done by those who hold certain ideas, against those who hold others.

It is tempting to pause, at this point, and to ask whether ideas and culture are so related to race or blood that they depend upon it for their origin, their existence and their survival. History does not seem to answer this question in the affirmative. So far as its records go, ideas appear to be independent of racial stock. Some of the best ideas which belong to the legacy of ancient Greek culture were imported into the Greek world by men of Semitic stock, such as Zeno, the founder of Stoicism. But the real question which we have to face goes deeper than this. It is a question which continues to confront us whether we hold that ideas are appanages of blood, or are independent of blood. It is the question whether I have any moral claim that only persons of my own blood, or my own ideas, or my own blood *and* my own ideas, should count as my equals. It is the question whether the State is entitled to assume that I have such a claim, and, on the basis of such an assumption, to pass laws which turn my claim into a legal right, so that henceforth persons of different blood, or different ideas, or different blood and ideas, will be treated as legally unequal. These are moral questions; and they bring us back, once more, to the moral foundations of politics. No doubt, in the early history of humanity, there were such things as blood-groups and clan-States. No doubt, in early times, moral claims and legal rights were based on community of blood and membership of the clan. But in the long travail of our moral development we have long transcended such limitations. Community to-day is wider than consanguinity. We cannot pen moral claims and duties within the bounds of blood and kinship: we cannot limit the State, which is the minister and servant of those claims and duties, within the circle of race. The modern community is based not on consanguinity, but on contiguity. Our duties—our moral duties, and therefore also our legal duties, which spring from them—are duties to our neighbours, and to all our neighbours. It matters not whether our neighbours are Jew or Gentile, barbarian, Scythian, bond or free. My neighbour, when he is once my neighbour, has a moral claim to be treated as equal, and a moral claim to be treated as free, which cannot be simply overborne by differences of blood, and can only be qualified by differences of blood, in any way or in any degree, when a strong and grave moral counter-claim for such qualification has been established. It is just possible that, in a new colonial community of different bloods or races which are still very separate and heterogeneous, some genuine claim to qualification of the moral claims of equality and freedom may be established. It is just possible—in such a community. But it is equally possible that, even there, men may cheat themselves into discovering a claim when there is none; and at any rate in our old European communities, in which men have lived together as neighbours for centuries, the plain and undiluted principle of my duty to my neighbour stands clear and unqualified.

I have lingered long over these physical considerations of breed and race. Let me now turn from these physical foundations of politics to what I called, in the beginning of my argument, the economic and the psychological. Here there are two current and congenial doctrines which claim our attention. One is the doctrine of economic materialism. The other is the doctrine of social utilitarianism.

The doctrine of economic materialism, as it was taught by Marx, starts from the matter on which man labours, in his capacity of a wealth-getting animal, and the methods by which, under the influence and compulsion of that matter, he applies his labour. The matter on which man labours, according to this doctrine, is a developing or evolutionary matter, which from age to age unfolds new possibilities, dictates new methods of labour, and imposes new ways of the acquisition of wealth. In any given age, and in any given society, the way in which that society is then acquiring its wealth determines its life, and constitutes the foundation of its politics. We have thus a moving foundation; but the foundation is itself inevitably determined by the movement of economic matter, so that it has to be what it is at any given point of the process of movement; and just as the foundation is itself inevitably determined, so again it determines, with the same inevitability, the society, the State and the system of politics appropriate to itself, so that they, too, have to be what they are at any given moment of time. If the argument stopped at this point, we should not only be furnished with foundations of politics, but we should also be tied to them like Prometheus to his rock. We should be bound, as Aeschylus says, in the 'unbreakable fetters of adamantine chains'. But the argument goes further, and suffers a change. At a certain point in the movement which has been described as inevitable the free will of man is introduced, and, with it, the idea of a duty towards which that free will should consciously direct its effort. When the change in the ways of the acquisition of wealth has at length produced an organised labouring class, called the proletariat, the hour has struck for voluntary action. The leaders of that class, whether produced by it, or coming from outside it to espouse its claims, will summon it to vindicate those claims by its own effort, and to do so by establishing a new society in which they will be realised. Proletarian man will thus tear himself loose at last from the rock of necessity, which after all was only a moving rock that shifted with the development of economic matter and the consequent evolution of the ways of acquiring wealth. He will base himself and his social life and his system of politics on claims which are henceforth immutable—the claim to be a free agent in the process of production: the claim to be an equal partner in the process of distribution: the general claims which flow from his intrinsic moral nature as proletarian man.

There is a fundamental dualism in the doctrine of economic materialism. It begins with the self-determination of matter; it ends in the self-determination of man. It begins by basing politics on the foundation of material necessity: it ends by basing politics on the foundation of moral claims. The real passion, and the real power, of economic materialism is not its materialism: it is rather, if we may use that word, its moralism. Socialist thinkers have tried to find a foundation for a cause which is ultimately a moral cause in a non-moral doctrine of economic necessity, which leads them to argue that the necessary development of economic matter must inevitably produce the result which they desire. In reality the foundation is only, at most, a buttress; in other words, it only supports, or is supposed to support, a cause which is really based on the true and sure foundation of the moral claims of working men and women to a greater liberty and a larger equality. The danger of the buttress is that it does not really support —on the contrary it may even weaken—the cause which it is supposed to establish. If economic necessity could actually be counted upon to produce the victory of the cause—and that is the contention advanced—why should its votaries do anything to promote the victory, and why should they not rather fold their hands in tranquil expectation? There is no good and sufficient answer to that question; and thus we are led to see that not only is the supposed foundation only, at most, a buttress, or rather a supposed buttress, but the supposed buttress is also, in reality, an obstacle to the cause which it seems to support. A cause which is based on moral claims needs the support of moral effort; and moral effort is the opposite of economic necessity, and is hindered and injured by any reliance upon it.

The argument here advanced is not an argument against socialism. It is only an argument against the foundation of economic materialism on which many socialist thinkers have tried to base their cause. They are not true to their own foundation; and they really imply, when they develop their views, a different foundation, which I am perfectly willing to accept and indeed have been seeking, all along, to defend. This is the foundation of moral claims, issuing in moral effort. To-day, in our Western world, new moral claims of working men, and working women, are beginning to be felt and acknowledged by tender and sensitive consciences. The more widely, and the more deeply, they are felt and acknowledged, the greater becomes the sense of our moral obligation to our neighbours. A new emotion—and moral obligation must always be tinged by emotion if it is to be a matter of real recognition and genuine acknowledgment of claims—is added to our lives. On the foundation of this greater sense of moral obligation—this new emotion, if I may use that word, intending by it nothing sentimental, but that deep and ultimate feeling which we experience towards whatsoever things are honest and just in the world of morals, just as we experience it towards whatsoever things are lovely in the world of art—on this foundation, which is a new foundation for our age, we have to rebuild our politics. We have to turn these new moral claims, in some respects and to some extent, into legal rights: we have to turn our new recognition and acknowledgment, in some respects and to some extent, into legal duties. I cannot say in what exact respects, and to what exact extent, this should be done, or will be done. Time and tentative effort alone can give the answer. I am no advocate of political revolution. If I were, I should not speak of time and tentative effort. But I believe that there are such things as moral revolutions. I believe that we are now undergoing such a revolution in our sense of moral obligation and in our moral emotions. I am anxious that we should be conscious of what we are undergoing, and ready for the political changes—the changes in legal rights and legal duties—which are necessarily involved in the fact of moral progress. The moral foundation of politics is always the same, but it is always changing. In that it is like the coral reef, which is always the same, and always different. But the change which is growth is only the affirmation of identity. Even if England should move, in the strength of a greater sense of moral obligation, to a new socialist commonwealth, she would still be the same by virtue of moving in the strength of the same fundamental sense. It is only States which, like the old autocratic State in Russia, were not based on the sense of moral obligation that must be utterly overthrown before that sense can find a political structure to express and fulfil its demands.

There is another doctrine which still asks a hearing—the doctrine of social utilitarianism. This is the doctrine which, as I have said, assumes that the foundations of politics are psychological foundations. The ultimate, on this view, is the satisfaction of wants or desires, and therefore of the needs or interests which provoke these wants or desires; and these wants or desires are regarded as inhering not so much in individuals (though they will, of course, be felt by individuals) as in social classes which are driven by social interests or needs to social wants or desires. We are thus face to face with a socialised form of the old individualistic utilitarianism, which has turned, as it were, a somersault, and come down on the opposite side. In this new form of utilitarianism it is social groups or classes which become the centres of pleasurable or painful sensation: it is the satisfaction of group-desires for pleasurable sensation, and of group-dislikes of painful sensation, which becomes the foundation of politics and the controlling purpose of law. Now such a form of belief may run in two different directions. If one direction is followed, the attempt will be made to satisfy exclusively the wants of the one greatest group, without regard to the wants of the others. We shall thus arrive, by another route than that of economic materialism, at the same philosophy of the proletarian State which is preached by the economic materialists. We shall have a State founded and grounded on the wants of the proletarian class only, regardless of the wants and desires of other classes. The difficulty of that consummation is its obvious partiality; and even if we defend that partiality on the ground that it serves to correct a previous partiality in favour of the other side, we do not escape the difficulty by our defence. The other direction in which the doctrine of social utilitarianism may run seems more promising. If this other direction be followed, the attempt will be made to satisfy the wants of *all* social groups—so far as they can all be satisfied simultaneously. Each set of wants will then be satisfied, in some degree and to some extent: no set of wants will be satisfied altogether. This involves a complicated effort of 'social engineering'. Can such social engineering be successful, and can conflicting wants—for the wants of the different groups must necessarily conflict—be simultaneously satisfied? The difficulty with which we are faced may be stated in a dilemma. Either the State will become, in its actual practice, an organ for the satisfaction of the wants of property-owners and the professional classes, in which case it will not satisfy proletarian wants, and will be destitute of foundation for those who feel those wants; or it will become an organ for the satisfaction of proletarian wants, in which case it will not satisfy the wants of the other social groups, and will be destitute of foundation for those who feel those wants. We may, of course, seek to deny the existence of the dilemma: we may urge that the State should stand supreme over conflicting wants, and should engineer a *via media*. But if wants are the masters of the State, and the foundation on which it is built, how can it stand supreme over wants? When we make social wants the foundation of the State, we make the State the servant of social wants. It is a servant, and not a master; and it is a servant who is bound to serve two masters—or more than two. Now if it be true that no man can serve two masters, but either he will hate the one and love the other, or else hold to the one and despise the other, it follows that when we enthrone social wants as masters of the State we turn the State, in effect, into the servant of one social want.

This result may well make us shy of regarding social wants as the masters of the State and the foundation of politics. We all of us, in our hearts, desire a State which will be the master and not the servant of social wants—a State which can adjust, compose and control such wants. A State can only discharge that great office if it acts in the name of a principle superior to social wants. If it acts in the name of such a principle, it is the servant of that principle. I should therefore say that the State can only be master in the conflict of social wants if it acts as the servant of some final principle, some ultimate foundation, which enables it to control the conflict. That principle and foundation is moral obligation. I quoted, when I began, Kant's saying that true politics cannot take a single step forward unless it has first done homage to morals. I recur to the saying as I end. We need some criterion for the State, some master of the State, some foundation of the State, other than wants. Wants, in themselves and by themselves, are infinite, immeasurable, unadjustable. They can only be made finite, measurable and adjustable by something beyond themselves. It is not what a man, or a class of men, *wants* in the world of material satisfactions that is the measure and criterion for the State. It is what a man, or a class of men, *claims*, and the rest of us acknowledge, in the world of moral obligation. When I feel, in my conscience, the pull of such a claim on me—the claim (shall I say, in simple words) for a fair deal in this brief mortal life—I do two things: first, as a private individual, I acknowledge my responsibility for meeting that claim by my private action, and next, as a citizen, I acknowledge my responsibility, and that of all my fellow-citizens, for

meeting it through the public action of the State, which
will then turn the claim, in some respects and to some
extent, into a legal right which it is our legal duty to
respect and realize. To acknowledge responsibility as a
private individual means moral obligation. To acknowledge responsibility as a citizen means political obligation.
The second of these two things is an extension of the first;
an outcrop of the first: a building erected on the foundation of the first. I shall make the point clearer if I add a
further remark. We are apt to think that political obligation—that is to say, responsibility for fulfilling legal duty
—is an obligation to the State, to the law of the State, to
the Government of the State which declares and enforces
law. So, immediately, it is; but ultimately it is something
more. It is an obligation to my fellow-citizens, an obligation to behave to them as they have a legal right that
I should. The State is really a mediator. Fundamentally,
I do not so much owe obligation *to* it as I owe obligation
through it; and my ultimate obligation is always an obligation to my fellow-citizens. If I pay taxes to the State
which the State expends on social services for the benefit
of my less fortunate fellow-citizens, I am really paying to
them, and as a matter of duty to *them*. When we look at
matters in this light, we can see that political obligation
is the same sort of thing as moral obligation; that it is
based upon it; that it is a sort of extension or outcrop
of it; that it would not exist without it. The ultimate
reason why I come to owe legal duties to my fellow-
citizens is the fact that I start by owing, and acknowledging,
a moral duty to my neighbour. And the ultimate function
of the State, which enforces legal duties, is the function of

servant to that ground of moral obligation from which those duties spring.

Moral obligation is the final rock. I do not ask how it came to exist: that question is fully enough discussed in Bergson's recent book on the two sources of morality and religion. I simply assume that moral obligation exists; and assuming its existence I say that it is the foundation of politics; that it inspires and dictates all that the State does; and again that it controls and limits everything that it does. For the State which is untrue to moral obligation—which contravenes it by contravening moral claims and responsibilities, such as the claims to be treated as free and as equal, and the responsibilities for meeting those claims— such a State is not on the rock, and it will not stand.

VIII
THE TEACHING OF POLITICS

Delivered before the University of London Institute of Education, 8 June 1936

You might think that, being a professor of political science, I come here to plead for the teaching of political science in schools—at any rate in the abbreviated and attenuated form known as civics, which is defined in the *New English Dictionary* as 'that part of political science which is concerned with the rights and duties of citizenship'. Not a bit of it. I will not say that I come to you with an open mind (everybody says that, and it generally means a mind hermetically sealed); but I will say that I come to you with a mind full of doubts about the place of political science in a university, and still more clouded with doubts about its place in the school. Indeed, I doubt whether it has *any* place in the school. Political science, in its full sense, is too difficult; and that, I think, for two reasons. In the first place, it has too few certainties. Its premisses are uncertain; its conclusions are dubious. Each professor of political science is apt to feel about the other professors, if not about himself, that they argue from questionable axioms, by a still more questionable process of logic, to conclusions that are almost unquestionably wrong. The layman, even more sceptical, is inclined to adopt towards political science the attitude of Mrs Prig to the Mrs Harris so often mentioned by Mrs Gamp: 'I don't believe there's no sich a subject'. Sir Herbert Samuel, president of the Institute of Philosophy, when he took the chair lately at a lecture by a professor of political science (in fact, by myself) confessed to that attitude. A subject that either doesn't exist, or, if it exists, can give only a dusty answer to the schoolboy hot for certainty, is not a subject for the schoolboy. In the second place, speaking more seriously, I would say that the study of political science is beyond the capacity, or rather, beyond the range of experience, of the schoolboy—even of the schoolboy nearing the end of a secondary school career. Let me quote some words which I wrote a little time ago.

The study of politics is more akin to the study of ethics than it is to the study of Latin or mathematics or history. It requires some previous experience of life. Before you can really study the theory of good and evil in ethics, you must have felt their tussle in your own conscience: you must have realised, in your own life, the existence of moral problems. Similarly before you can really study the theory of right and wrong in politics, you must have undergone some sort of political experience: you must have felt what it is like to be confronted with some sort of political issue; you must have wrestled yourself, in some way, with the problems of conduct and organisation which arise in human societies.

You will see what I had in mind when I wrote those words. Political philosophy (note that I have changed my term, and ask yourselves why I have) is allied to ethics, and, indeed, is a sort of ethics. It is a study of the ethics of an organised community—a study of the things men ought to do and forbear from doing in the life of an organised community, as those things appear in the light of a pre-vious knowledge (and not only knowledge, but also experience) of the things men ought to do and forbear from doing in their individual lives. Now just as you can't teach ethics to the schoolboy, in the sense of a philosophy of the principles of individual conduct and the basis of those principles, so you can't teach politics to him either, in the sense of a philosophy of the principles of community-conduct and the basis of those principles. You may give him, indeed, in the field of individual conduct, some ethical drill, or, as Aristotle called it, some moral habituation; but that is practice rather than philosophy. So again you may give him, in the field of community-conduct, some civic drill or political habituation; but that, too, if it can be given at all, is practice rather than philosophy. If you try to give to a boy moral and political philosophy—the study of the ultimate principles of conduct—you are giving him something he can't digest, but can only regurgitate and repeat. You are expecting him to do at 16 or 17 what belongs to 21+. It is one of the dangers of places of education that they are tempted to expect from an early age what belongs to another and a later. It is a real danger. If a boy is prematurely fed with unrealised generalisations, unrelated to his experience, he is being gorged rather than fed. The clever boy who is willing, because he is taught, to accept and proclaim some general theorem which he has not understood is on the way to intellectual dishonesty. He is getting near to the lie in the soul.

I banish political science from the school; but can I leave room for civics? This is, you will remember, 'that part of political science which is concerned with the rights and duties of citizenship'. It is a part which looks terribly like the whole; for when you have dealt with the rights and duties of citizenship, you have laid the foundations and built the ground floor, and the rest is just superstructure.

But let us stop and think. Is civics really a *part* of political science (or of political philosophy, as I should prefer to call the subject), or does it stand in some different relation from that of part, and is it an ally or companion rather than a part? I incline to answer the question in the second sense. I suggest—at any rate for the moment, and tentatively, though I may presently try to go back on the suggestion— that the teaching of civics, or what is called education for citizenship, perhaps stands to the teaching of political philosophy in the same sort of relation in which practical ethical drill stands to the teaching of moral philosophy. Now practical ethical drill, or education for goodness, is different from the teaching of moral philosophy, though it is related to it; and in the same way it is possible that practical civic drill, or education for citizenship, is different from the teaching of political philosophy, though it is related to it. I think there is something in the distinction I am trying to draw, and I want to put it before you. Every good schoolmaster tries to educate for goodness without putting ethics into the curriculum. He does it imperceptibly and indirectly, or, as Blake says, 'silently, invisibly'—through the history lesson, through the literature lesson, through all lessons; in the playground; everywhere—but he does not 'seek to tell his love, love that never told can be'...at any rate to youth of that tender age. Is something of the same sort true of education for citizenship? Cannot one try to give it without putting civics into the curriculum? Is it, or can it be made, just a practical drill, flowering out of all subjects, or at any rate out of a number of subjects, but not demanding a subject to itself? Can we follow the way of Blake here too, and act 'silently, invisibly'? Not altogether, perhaps. You can put courage or the spirit of fair play into a boy without his knowing the great injection you have made. Perhaps you can't put a sense of civic duty into him without telling him something about civic institutions, or the spirit of civic fairness and tolerance without telling him something about political parties and the part they all have to play in the democratic method of government by discussion. It may be, after all, that education for citizenship is different from education for goodness, in that it involves some special substance or content of teaching, even if that substance or content be taught descriptively only and not philosophically. The moral conscience in all of us can respond of itself to a quiet and silent invitation. Perhaps the civic conscience needs feeding before it can respond— feeding with descriptive matter; feeding with some account of the institutions and forces among which it will be called on to play. We will wait and see, as the argument proceeds, which way the balance lies. For the moment let us assume that we have advanced one step. We have come to the conclusion that education for citizenship may be a sort of practical drill—at any rate in one aspect, though it may also have others—analogous in its way to, though in some respects different from, the practical drill involved in education for goodness. That is a thing worth thinking about. There is also another thing, also worth thinking about, which is possibly connected with this conclusion. Perhaps education for citizenship is not so much parallel to education for goodness as just a part of it —just an aspect of it—just a flowering of it in one particular way. Perhaps a master or mistress need not say,

'Here are two compartments: now I must get into one, and give practical ethical drill; now I must get into the other, and give practical civic drill'. Perhaps the two compartments are mansions in a single house; and civics, properly understood, runs into, or comes out of, ethics. Kant said, long ago, that a true theory of politics must begin by doing homage to ethics.

But I want to pause at this point in order to face, and to try to solve, a dilemma in which we seem to be involved by the very notion of education for citizenship—especially if it be understood as a sort of practical drill. Notice the word citizenship, and notice that it is, by its very nature, connected with the idea of the State. When you notice that, you begin to see the dilemma. If you educate for citizenship, you educate for the State, and for good membership of the State. That, for reasons we shall see in a moment, is a terrifying idea. On the other hand, if you *don't* educate for citizenship, and *don't* educate for the State, you are inviting trouble—at any rate when your State is a democratic State, demanding thought and intelligence from its members, and when your State is confronted, as it is to-day, by complicated problems of economic planning within, and of international policy without, which crave the wariest of walking.

Take the first horn of the dilemma. 'If you educate for citizenship', I said, 'you educate for the State, and for good membership of the State.' 'That', I also said, 'is a terrifying idea.' Why should it be terrifying? Why shouldn't we embrace the idea of Aristotle, expressed in the first sentence of the eighth book of his *Politics*, that 'the citizen should be moulded to suit the form of government under which he lives'? Well, there are two things I would say in regard to that matter. First, it is an old English bugbear, as old as 1760 or older, that the State should take over education and adjust it to its needs. The State had no more right to educate children, Priestley said in 1768, than it had to fix their dress; national education, said Godwin in 1793, ought uniformly to be discouraged on account of its obvious alliance with national government. It was the terror of Nonconformists, the terror of Radicals, the terror of all thoughtful English individualists, and even of good sober Anglicans, that the State should grasp the child and indoctrinate the young mind. In spite of that terror we have managed to get a system of national education; but we have only got it, and slowly at that, because we have also managed to keep national education, in the actual content and process of teaching, independent of national government. Now what will happen if we begin to make civics, and training for citizenship, part of the content and part of the process of teaching? Can we keep it out of the hands of national government? Can we say, 'We teachers, independently, of our own motion, on our own lines, will give the teaching which *we* think that our system of national government requires'? Or will the national government be tempted to say, 'I know what is required for my needs, and *I* will take a hand'? We may hope, and we may believe, that the first alternative will prevail; but we must face the fact that if a political party finds that teaching in civics of which it disapproves is being given in schools, and if that political party acquires a majority in Parliament and forms a government, such a government may be compelled to take a hand in this matter. That brings me to the second thing I want to say in regard to Aristotle's dictum about the moulding of the citizen to suit the form of government under which he lives. We must not only look at our English experience: we must also look at the experience of the Continent. Anybody who has looked, as I have tried to look, at the history-readers of Nazi Germany, or the elementary primers of Fascist Italy (I bought one of the latter for my little boy of three, and we have often looked at it together in the early morning, when he awaked, as he tends to do, at a remarkably early hour)—anybody who has done that receives a shock. The government *has* taken a hand. It is prescribing the content and process of teaching. It is doing what nearly all of us in England don't want done. We in England draw a distinction between the right, or duty, of the State to provide and supervise the administrative cadre of education, and the right or duty of the teacher to provide and conduct, spontaneously and autonomously, the content and process of the actual education given. It is a most important distinction; and it is a distinction which you, Sir, have taught me to appreciate.[1] May we not begin to impair that distinction—to rub it away—to blunt its edge—if we begin to import civics into the content and process of our teaching? If that is the price we pay for the importation, is the commodity we get worth the price? Such fears may be fanciful. But even if they are fanciful, they had better be expressed.

But now let us take the second horn of the dilemma. 'If you *don't* educate for citizenship,' I said, 'and if you

[1] The chairman who presided at the lecture was Sir Percy Nunn.

don't educate for the State, you are inviting trouble—at any rate when your State is a democratic State, and when that State is confronted by complicated problems.' A democratic system of government is not an automatism, which revolves of its own mechanical self. It will only produce anything if you put your heart, and still more, your mind, into it, and it will produce as much (and no more) as you put of your heart, and still more, of your mind, into it. Now you can't put your mind into it unless you know what it is into which you are putting your mind, and unless you have some mind—some trained and experienced and properly prepared mind—to put into it. That is a reason—and it is an unanswerable sort of reason —for doing something, whatever dangers there may possibly be in the doing of it. And that something, we now begin to see, is not merely a practical civic drill, analogous to, or flowering out of, practical moral drill: it is not merely an appeal to the heart, if I may use that word 'heart': it also involves a theoretic or intellectual discipline, and it is also an appeal to the mind, an informing of the mind, a preparing of the mind. If in our schools we are, as we believe, preparing children for life by giving them the basic minimum knowledge of its forces and factors, and by furnishing them with the vitally necessary curiosities about it which will serve them as hooks of apprehension when they come to grapple with it—if we are preparing children for life, we must also prepare them for the life political. We must give them the basic minimum knowledge of the forces and factors of that life—of its institutions; of the problems which have to be solved by means of those institutions—and we must furnish them betimes with the curiosities about it which will enable them to grapple with it.

There are the two horns of the dilemma. We have to find some sort of seat between them on which we can sit in comfort. I will try to provide such a seat for myself by indulging in three reflections.

The first reflection turns on the word citizenship. It is education for citizenship of which I am speaking. Now we often use the words citizenship and citizen loosely; but I want to take them *stricto sensu*. When we speak of citizenship, or at any rate when I talk of citizenship, it is the democratic State that is intended. Any education of the citizen in the democratic State is not an education of him to suit the government; it is an education of him to be the government—or at any rate to make the government, to inspire it, to control it. We must educate our masters, as somebody said after the Second Reform Bill, though I have never quite understood who the 'we' were who were to educate our masters, or what the distinction really was, and I should prefer to say, 'We must educate ourselves to be masters'. In other words, education for citizenship is really a process of self-education for the proper performance of the right and duty, which belongs to us all, of helping to make, inspire, and control the government of our country.

That brings me to a second reflection. This process of education for citizenship, which is in its essence a process of self-education, and not a process of imposed education intended to adapt us to something other than ourselves, or above ourselves—this process is not confined to schools, though it has, of course, its place in schools, a place I shall presently seek to examine and discuss. Men educate themselves for citizenship by doing as well as learning. Or perhaps I should put my point better if I said, 'Men educate themselves for citizenship by what they do to educate themselves when they have ceased to be educated by others'. What I have in mind is membership of voluntary bodies—clubs, tutorial classes, trade unions, community associations on the new municipal housing estates, village institutes, churches and chapels and the various social groups that spring up round churches and chapels—all that rich growth of voluntary associations which is part of our lives as much as the State, and which can prepare us, by its experience, for the life of the State. By joining these bodies—and it should be one of the fruits of our school-education that we are encouraged to join them, and encouraged to feel that it is our duty to serve them—we shall learn in small what we have to do in large...not that participation in the discussions, the work, the experience of these bodies is really so small a thing, even in comparison with participation in the discussions, the work, the experience of the State, large as that may seem to be. There is also another thing to be said which may carry us even further. How is that body of public opinion made which inspires and controls the democratic State, and in the making of which (or at any rate in helping to make it) true citizenship consists? Isn't it largely, very largely, made in these voluntary bodies—clubs, trade unions, churches, chapels, community associations, village institutes...I had almost added, village public-houses, reflecting that, in my experience, they too can be a forum of debate, like the agora of ancient Athens, or the forum of ancient Rome? If that be so, to join these bodies, to participate in their life, to come out into the open and to join in uttering what the old Greeks called the 'word said into the middle' (τὸ λεγόμενον εἰς τὸ μέσον)—this is not only education for citizenship, but also the actual practice of citizenship. My own active citizenship—and, I venture to think, that of most of my hearers—is exercised in this way: by what I say in discussion clubs, by the letters I write to the papers, by whatever word I say into the middle while trying to help in the formation of public opinion. Do not let us have too narrow or pedantic a notion of citizenship. It isn't only attending political meetings, or voting in a polling booth, or getting elected to the Town Council, or even getting elected to Parliament. It is saying good and considered words into the middle, in any group and on any occasion where it is possible. Euripides said that long ago, and John Milton translated what he said, and put it in the forefront and as the motto of his *Areopagitica*:

> This is true liberty, when free-born men
> Having to advise the public may speak free.

I have still a third reflection which I need in order to get a comfortable seat between the horns of the dilemma. It is a reflection about education in schools--about education proper, in the strict sense of the term—about formal and regular education, such as is given to us by others, our pastors and masters, in the plastic days of our youth. What I want to say about that is simple. Education for citizenship may be a part of such education—it *is* a part of such education—but it is only a part, and not the greatest part. Education is education of the whole man, who is not exhausted in his citizenship (far from it); who is a member of all sorts of voluntary bodies as well as of the State; and who, over and above that, and beyond that, is his own individual self and a living soul. We must not get civics, and education in civics, in a wrong perspective, or be too eager about what I may call the civicising of our youth. The first and greatest thing is their humanising. I was reading the other day a review of a volume of essays entitled *Education of To-day*. The reviewer commended an essay by the Headmaster of Winchester upon education in citizenship, and especially his dictum that education for citizenship is a secondary end of high importance, but not the primary end of education. The reviewer went on to add, 'The tendency to make it such is apparent in much modern educational practice, and it is potentially a very dangerous one.' For myself, I am not sure that any great danger has yet been incurred; but I do see the possibility of danger. The danger is that of treating the young as means—means to a greater and finer England: chosen instruments for the setting of Jerusalem in this land. Well, it is their duty to do what they can for that consummation; but the fact remains, the ultimate fact, that they are ends —ends in themselves. We educate them to be that; and therefore we educate each of them to be a whole man— not *miles pro patria*, nor even *civis pro civitate*, but a whole man. To be a whole man is to be a lover of truth because it is truth, and just for its own sake—a lover of the rigour of scholarship, whether in letters or science. To be a whole man is to be a lover of beauty because it is beauty, and just for its own sake—a lover of good and noble literature, or good and noble music, or any good and noble form of art.[1] Civic training has its place; but it is secondary to these things. If civic training be pressed to the detriment of humanity, in the highest and finest sense of that word —and that is what seems to me to be happening in Germany—it will go badly with our Universities, as I think it is going badly in Germany, and it will go badly with our national culture. I know there are some in our Universities who already fear civics as a rival or danger to scholarship. My old school at Manchester had no civics in the eighteen-eighties; but we threw up, in my time, a Lord Chief Justice, a Head of the Treasury, a great journalist, and one or two other civic beings. Perhaps, with the cussedness of human nature, one takes more to

[1] Here the lecturer paused and said, as the memory of his school-days from 1888 to 1893 came suddenly into his mind, 'I cannot but stop, at this point, to recall the memory of two teachers, both now dead, to whom I owe an unforgettable debt. One had been a scholar of Trinity College, Cambridge, and a pupil, I think, of the great Shilleto. He taught me the niceties of οὐ μή and μὴ οὐ, and the subtleties of Goodwin's *Greek Moods and Tenses*. He instilled a love of Greek, and a sense for the Greek language, which has never died, and which has coloured and strengthened whatever I have done since in other fields. I salute the memory of my master *in litteris Graecis*. The other had been a scholar of Trinity College, Oxford. He was a man of delicate and refined taste, a lover of pure English, alive to all the beauty of both English and classical literature. Under him we learned by heart passages of Euripides and Virgil, sonnets of Shakespeare and Wordsworth, poems of Shelley, and chapters of Isaiah. We not only learned the words: we also learned to feel the sense, the emotion, the suggestion, the beauty. He too left me a legacy that has not been lost or squandered. I still repeat to myself, when I lie awake, or am wandering by myself along the roads, the passages he taught me to love; and still, in whatever I write, I bear some traces of his love of pure speech and pure writing. His memory, too, I salute. These were my masters, and this was my education, nearly fifty years ago.'

civics and politics if they have not been proclaimed or
practised at school, and if one comes to them fresh. At
any rate, it was so with me. And in any case I want to
keep room in our English places of education for what
Plato calls the philosopher—not the professor of philosophy, but the man who is curious and passionate about
ultimate things. I was reading a passage about these
philosophers the other day in the *Theatetus*. 'From their
youth upwards', says Plato, 'they know not the way to
the Agora, nor where the Law Court is, or the Council
Chamber, or any other place of common civic assembly.
Laws and regulations they neither see nor hear...of all
these things they are even ignorant that they are ignorant.'
Remember that it was Plato, the lover of politics and the
writer of the *Republic*, who wrote these words. He loved
civics, but he loved philosophy more; and he would not
have loved civics so much unless he had loved philosophy
more.

I seem to be a Balaam, constantly preaching the opposite
of what you would expect me to preach. I do not think
I am quite as bad as that. I only want to get this matter of
training for citizenship into perspective—to see its possible
dangers, and to suggest its necessary qualifications. It is
time, after seeing the dangers and suggesting the qualifications, to say something positive. I can see three lines along
which I might try to say something positive. One would
be the line of training for civic leadership—the training of
the statesman. Another would be the line of training for
civic administration—the training of the civil servant,
local as well as national. The third is the line of training
for the ordinary civic duty of the ordinary citizen. If I

went down either of the first two lines I should never end. I will therefore confine myself to the third. Anyhow, it is my subject; and I ought to confine myself to it if I have any sense of relevance or decency.

I shall only speak of education for the ordinary civic duty of the ordinary citizen as such education is given, or may be given, in schools; but I would remind you that I have said that half of such education, or even more, can come, and does come, after school. But what of the school, and what of the things that can be done in the school? First, a master can give the civic incentive, just as he tries to give the moral incentive; and he can give it in the same quiet and unobtrusive way. It is said that a burnt child shuns the fire. It may also be said that a preached-at child shuns the thing which has been preached at him. These incentives, these practical drills, are matters for delicate handling and not for frontal attacks. Secondly, a master can give not only the incentive to civic action, but the necessary stuff of civic knowledge which is needed for wise civic action. This doesn't mean any teaching of political science. I ruled that out long ago. It doesn't mean any teaching of a separate subject called civics. I don't see room for that in the curriculum. Even if there were room, I don't see how such a subject is to be composed and constructed. If it is just descriptive of institutions, I fear that such description, for those who are not really curious and have not already some knowledge of what goes on inside institutions, will be a matter of hollow shells and empty husks. If it is rather a matter of the preaching of civic pride and civic duty—well, that, as I have just said, is a subtle matter which had better not be preached but insensibly insinuated. What I have in mind when I talk of the teaching of the necessary stuff of civic knowledge is something that will best come in, or flow out of, existing parts of the curriculum. It can be given in connection with English, geography, and history—at any rate if these subjects are not too much formalised and compartmentalised as separate specialisms. For example, one thing I greatly desire is a clear understanding of the use and abuse of political terms—justice, authority, liberty, equality, sovereignty, and all those blessed Mesopotamian words. The clear use of clear words, with definite meaning, is a civic duty. You can drive home that duty in connection with essay work, or the study of English, or the study of history. Another thing we should all want to see is some understanding of our institutions—social as well as political: the trade union as well as the cabinet—but of our institutions in connection with the things they have done and may be expected to do, and not as hollow shells. To understand institutions in that way is to understand them as part of the historic process and in the light of their historic setting—in other words, to understand them in history and as part of the study of history. Still a third thing we should all desire is some sense of current affairs— of the problems bequeathed to us by the living past, with their historic colour and historic roots. That again is a matter of history, and, it may be, fairly remote history. We must not think that the historic colour and the historic roots of our current problems are derived from the present century only. The Tudors are still with us, and Henry VIII is still alive.

What I have just said seems to throw a heavy burden

on the history teacher. It does. When you talk of education for citizenship, it is the teaching of history that is the crucial teaching. Here, as a teacher of history myself, I want to utter a warning to us poor teachers of history. Our danger, when we are trying to trace the roots of the present back to the past, and to make our history civically serviceable, is that we may modernise the past in order to show its connection with the present. It is true that the present always conceives the past largely from its own angle, and largely in its own terms; and from that point of view there are as many pasts as there are presents. But this must not be overdone. You may, for example, Hitlerise or totalitarianise Henry VIII in order to show an ancient root of modern dictatorship. But when you have done that, you have got him somehow askew. Having modernised the Tudor, you find you must re-Tudorise him. Truth is the ultimate in the teaching of history. The past is different from the present; and truth demands that it should be shown in its difference. When you teach history in terms of civics, you are making the past serve the present. When you teach it in terms of truth, you make the past an end in itself. Somehow we have to do both. Well, it is a difficult job—but *magna est veritas, et praevalere debet.*

One last word, down a totally new side-way, which isn't a side-way at all, but a great road that deserves an hour's exploration all to itself. If there is to be education for citizenship there must be an organisation of education —of our schools from the age of 5 to that of 18+ —which is itself civic, and suits the requirements of citizenship. Education for citizenship isn't only a matter of the civicisation of teaching: it is a matter of the organisation of the whole school, and of all schools, to suit a civic ideal. Now does it suit our ideal that we have still, as Dr Norwood has said, a division in our secondary education—the division 'between boarding-schools closed to all save the well-to-do, and day-schools open to all classes'—and that, as he has also said, 'we are in danger of producing two classes of citizen in this country'? I just throw out the question. And having done so I add that for those who are concerned with education for citizenship this is perhaps the gravest matter in English education to-day.

IX

MAITLAND AS A SOCIOLOGIST

Delivered before the Institute of Sociology, London, 17 March 1937

Frederic William Maitland, the grandson of Samuel Maitland, a historian of the Dark Ages who was famous a hundred years ago, was born in 1850 and died at the end of 1906. Educated at Eton and at Trinity College, Cambridge, he was called to the bar in 1876; but devoting himself to the study of law rather than its practice (as Jeremy Bentham had done before him), he came back to Cambridge in 1884 as Reader of English Law, and in 1888 he was elected Downing Professor of the Laws of England. In the twenty-two years of his teaching and writing in Cambridge, from the age of 34 to the age of 56, he achieved a volume of work, and accumulated a store of influence, which made him one of the great forces of his generation, and indeed a great force to-day. The wonder is all the greater when we reflect that he suffered from ill-health for the greater part of his working life, and, for the last eight years, was regularly compelled to fly to the South every winter. Perhaps the flame burned all the brighter because the vital reserves were always being summoned to feed the wick.

He was primarily a lawyer, or, more exactly, a legal historian. But he interpreted law in that broad and generous sense which makes it the general framework of social life—a framework partly created by the needs and aspirations of society, but partly, and in turn, reacting on those needs and aspirations, and helping to determine their form and their development. In this sense it may be said that the study of law was a thing which became in his hands a sociological study. He went beyond legal rules and procedure to the social content of law. Legal history became for him a history of the manor, regarded as a social institution or group; it became a history of township and borough, similarly regarded: it became, at the last, a history of the whole general institution which we call the group or society, in all its various forms.

In the last ten years of his life, from 1896 to 1906, he was more and more fascinated by the problem of the group. In 1897 he published *Domesday Book and Beyond*, in which he dealt with the society of the manor. In the autumn of 1897 I heard him deliver at Oxford, in a voice of which I have never forgotten the magic, some lectures on the societies of Township and Borough, which were published under that title in 1898. He had moved to the general problem of the group at large by 1900. In that year appeared a little volume, *The Political Theories of the Middle Age*, translated from Gierke's German, but armed with an introduction dealing with what I have called the general problem of the group, which perhaps exerted more influence, if not on legal, at any rate on general contemporary thought, than anything else which he wrote. It influenced the thought of Dr Figgis about the Church; it was cited by the Webbs in the introduction to the 1911 edition of their *History of Trade Unionism*: it was a mine for all who were interested in groups—groups ecclesiastical or groups economic or any manner of group.

But the little volume of 1900 was not the only publication of Maitland's last years which bore on this problem. He wrote a number of other essays and articles of which it was also the theme. Some were lectures or papers read to clubs; one was an article contributed to a German legal periodical; two were articles contributed to our own *Law Quarterly Review*. They were all collected in the third volume of his *Collected Papers*, which appeared in 1911. They have now been republished in a little volume, under the title of *Selected Essays*, which appeared at the end of last year. If one desires to find the quintessence of 'Maitland as a Sociologist', it is to be found in that volume, along with his introduction to *The Political Theories of the Middle Age*.

Before I turn to Maitland's theory of the group, which may be called his specific contribution to sociology, there is something which may properly be said, and indeed must necessarily be said, about the sociological method which he followed in the writing of legal and constitutional history. I have said 'the sociological method': I might more exactly, using a prefix of which the lawyers are fond, have said 'the quasi-sociological method', intending thereby a method which is not specifically sociological, but is the sort of method, or analogous to the sort of method, which would be used by the sociologist. What I mean is that Maitland interpreted the manor, and feudalism, and the Middle Ages in general, intrinsically and by their own light, as a sociologist would seek to do —not extrinsically and through the spectacles of a later and different age, which is what the historian may do when he is not imbued with a tincture of sociology. This, to my mind, is the difference between Maitland and Stubbs. Great as Stubbs was, he wrote his *Constitutional History of England* in spectacles—the spectacles of Victorian Liberalism, which are all the more curious on his nose when one remembers that he was a natural Tory. Maitland wore no spectacles. He saw the Middle Ages *sub specie temporum suorum*—in the light of their own social conditions and their own stock of social ideas. We may call this gift which he had the gift of sympathetic imagination; but it is more than that—it is the gift of a sympathetic *scientific* imagination, and the science which inspires the gift is the science of sociology. 'To make discoveries', he said, 'we must form new habits of mind, and the thoughts of men in the past must once more become thinkable to us.' This leads me to another of his sayings, which I have never forgotten (though I quote it purely from memory, and therefore probably misquote it), that to understand the Middle Ages we must think ourselves back into a mediæval haze. 'Too often', he wrote, in words which express the idea behind that saying with a measured exactitude, 'we allow ourselves to suppose that, could we but get back to the beginning, we should find that all was intelligible, and should then be able to watch the process whereby simple ideas were smothered under technicalities and subtleties. But it is not so. Simplicity is the outcome of technical subtlety: it is the goal, not the starting-point. As we go backwards, the familiar outlines become blurred; the ideas become fluid, and instead of the simple we find the indefinite.'

This line of thinking and of interpretation brought many revolutions. You will all remember Maine's *Ancient*

Law and Maine's theory of the patriarchal origin of society. What has Maitland to say? 'Maine's patriarch, who is a trustee, who represents a corporation, looks to me suspiciously modern. He may be a savage, but he is in full evening dress.' That is one thing he had to say: and it is devastating. There was also another. He held that there was no one sort of origin, and no one sort of sequence of development. 'When this evidence about barbarians gets into the hands of men who...have been taught by experience to look upon all the social phenomena as interdependent, it begins to prove far less than it used to prove. Each case begins to look very unique, and a law which deduces that "mother right" cannot come after "father right", or that "father right" cannot come after "mother right", or which would establish any similar sequence of "states", begins to look exceedingly improbable.' Maitland was deeply convinced of the truth that there was no one line of progress, and that human societies did not grow logically by similar or identical processes of immanent development. Societies were interdependent: there was always a process of the diffusion of culture from one society to another: one society, borrowing from another which was an advance of itself, might make a sudden leap which would be inexplicable except in terms of such diffusion and borrowing. 'Our Anglo-Saxon ancestors did not arrive at the alphabet or at the Nicene Creed by traversing a long series of "stages": they leapt to the one and the other.'

I may seem to have strayed into anthropology, and to have taken Maitland with me in my straying. Let me return to history which is more indubitably history, and let me refer you to Maitland's treatment of feudalism. There are, he says, still some historians who talk of feudalism as if it were a disease of the body politic. Well, no doubt there were some things in the Middle Ages, things properly called feudal, which came of evil and made for evil. But take feudalism as a whole; use the term in a wide sense (as a sociologist would); and how does it appear? 'If we use the term in this wide sense, then (the barbarian conquests being given to us as an unalterable fact) feudalism means civilisation, the separation of employment, a division of labour, the possibility of national defence, the possibility of art, science, literature, and learned leisure; the cathedral, the scriptorium, the library, are as truly the work of feudalism as is the baronial castle.' Here is a thing which seems to me well said. It shows how the history of law became in Maitland's hands, as Mr Fisher has said, 'a contribution to the general history of human society'. The same lesson appears when we look at his account of one of the institutions of feudalism (in the wide sense of the word), the mediæval manor. How did it come to pass that the villagers followed that curious system of scattered strips in the three great open fields of arable land which surrounded their village dwellings? Had a lord done all this planning and parcelling? Hardly. How would it suit his interest, and how could he induce stubborn villagers to accept his ruling? Does it not look as if the body of villagers wanted each member to take the rough with the smooth, and no man to get off better than any other? They did not mind if this made cultivation difficult and diminished their returns. 'They sacrificed the cause of efficiency on the altar of equality.' There is insight into the nature of man, and especially into the nature of village society, in that epigram.

But it is time that I turned to what I have called Maitland's specific contribution to sociology—his general theory of the group. I have said that the theory of the group was engaging his attention in the last ten years of his life. I always remember one sentence (I think it recurred more than once) in those lectures on Township and Borough which I attended in 1897. 'Borough community is corporate: village community is not.' The question of the nature of corporativeness, if I may use that word, was stirring his mind. What, he was asking himself, is a group or a society of men, at its highest point of identity, when it is somehow one and the plurality of its members is somehow merged into the unity of one body —one *corpus* or corporation? That is a question which you cannot answer without ranging up and down the scale, from the loosest of cohesions to the tightest of corporations. Where does the change come—the magical change that gives you the corporate body? In what does the change consist, and who is it that produces the change? Is it the authority of the State and the fiat of the *princeps*? Or do corporations make themselves, and do they become what they are by their own proper motion?

It was partly the reading of Gierke's great book on the German *Genossenschaft* which had stimulated these questionings. It was partly also some issues which were being raised in this island about 1900. One of them was the Scottish Church case, which began in 1900 and was finally decided by the House of Lords, so far as the law of the matter went, in 1904. This was a case which raised the question of the identity of a Church. Another issue was that of the legal position of Trade Unions—the question whether a Trade Union was in any sense corporate and in any way liable therefore to be treated as a single body responsible for its acts and the acts of its agents—which was being raised in the English courts and led to the Taff Vale decision of 1901. But it was not only the reading of Gierke and the nature of contemporary events which stimulated Maitland's mind: it was also the course of his own study. He was dealing with the history of English law and English legal institutions. Now whatever else we may say about England, it has certainly been a paradise of groups. They begin in old Anglo-Saxon frith-gilds (mutual insurance societies, as I should call them, for the safer commission and the surer compensation of cattle-raids), if they are not even earlier than the frith-gilds: they continue, through mediæval religious gilds, mediæval societies of lawyers called Inns of Court, seventeenth-century Free Churches, seventeenth-century East India and other companies, down to modern groups such as Lloyd's, the Stock Exchange, the Trade Union, the London club (such as the Athenæum), and, as I am in private duty bound to mention, this Institute of Sociology which I am now addressing. These riches fascinated Maitland. They may well fascinate any Englishman. How shall we count them, and in what denominations and under what categories shall we classify them?

I have said that these riches fascinated Maitland. He told them over and over, from the far past to the multitudinous present with all its rapid and large increase of corporate or quasi-corporate groups. I cannot do better than quote Mr Fisher, his brother-in-law and biographer. 'Trade Unions and joint-stock companies, chartered boroughs and mediæval universities, village communities and townships, merchant guilds and crafts, every form of association known to mediæval or modern life came within his view, as illustrating the way in which English-men attempted "to distinguish and reconcile the manyness of the members and the oneness of the body". An enquiry of this kind was something entirely new in England.' I am not sure if it was entirely new—I remember, for example, Toulmin Smith's book on English Gilds—but it was certainly new in its scope, its zest, and its depth. Perhaps the fact that he was a member of Lincoln's Inn, and had worked in one of the old mediæval English legal societies, still living and active, and (what is more) had studied and written about the achievement of the lawyers who had also worked in these societies in bygone days—perhaps this stimulated his love for the theme of the group. Certainly he had a deep interest in the lawyer-group, which is a peculiar fact of our English life. (At any rate I know of nothing like our Inns of Court in any other country.) There is a lively passage about them, and the men who inhabited them during the Middle Ages, in the introduction which he wrote to a volume of the Year Books. 'They are gregarious, clubbable men, grouping themselves in hospices which become schools of law... arguing, learning, and teaching, the great mediators between life and logic, a reasoning, reasonable element in the English nation.'

A great mediator between life and logic—this is what Maitland himself was, when he dealt with the understanding of the group. The subject suited his own philosophical bent: he had been trained in the Mental and Moral Sciences Tripos, and had taken a first class in that Tripos in 1872. I am not sure that he did not lean too much to logic, at the expense of life, in his interpretation of the group at that highest point of its identity at which it becomes a corporation. He was affected by Gierke's theory: he thought that a corporation was a real person. He believed that the change which was reached in the scale of group-being, when you come to the corporation, was the emergence of a new person, with a mind and will of its own; and he believed that this person was real—as real, unless I am mistaken, as you and I are real. I cannot follow that interpretation; but I will not go into the reasons which hold me back from following. I have tried to explain them elsewhere.[1] Here I will only say that real group-persons terrify me, but leave me still a sceptic. When I am told, for instance, that the nation 'is an organism, with a being, ends, and means of action superior to those of the individuals, separate or grouped, who compose it' (and that is what I am told in the Italian Charter of Labour of 1927), I can only say that that is not what a nation is, or ever can be, to me. The group at its highest, when it almost seems to merge plurality into unity, is still to me so many individual human beings. What raises it to its highest is not the emergence of a real new personality, over and above the personalities of its members: it is simply the height or quality of the common purpose which individual persons agree in holding and

[1] *Introduction to Natural Law and the Theory of Society*, translated from Gierke, 1934.

willing—the width, the depth, and the permanence of that purpose. Purpose is all; and it is by their purposes that I should judge, range, classify, and also criticise, groups.

Having said these words, and having implied, as I confess that I have, that Maitland seems to me to have over-exalted the being of the corporate group, and to have contributed, in some measure, to the group-cult of our days (not that it is so marked in England as it is elsewhere), I now pass on—very gladly, and with far more zest in agreement than I have in my disagreement—to say some words about Maitland's contribution to the general understanding of our English groups and societies. There are two things which I wish to say. One concerns the idea of the group—and more particularly the corporate group, the group which acts as a single body or *corpus*, 'and moveth altogether if it move at all'—as it acts in the sphere of our national politics, or, in other words, in the sphere of the ·State. The other concerns the idea of the group—the group generally, corporate or unincorporate, whether it moves with the oneness of the body or the manyness of the members—as it acts in the sphere of our social life, or, in other words, in the sphere of Society.

In the sphere of our politics we have long had one idea of a corporation which seemed to Maitland curious, and indeed unfortunate. This is the idea of the king as a corporation sole, a corporation with only one member, to wit, himself. I would not necessarily dismiss altogether this idea of the corporation sole, curious as it may seem—though I do not like it in its particular application to the king. I have met and stayed with a corporation sole in

Massachusetts—Dr Lawrence Lowell, who is a corporation sole in respect of the Lowell Lectures, of which he holds the funds and for which he makes the arrangements. That corporation sole invited me to lecture, and paid me a generous remuneration: I have no quarrel with it. But I feel differently, taught by Maitland, about the idea of the king as a corporation sole. Dr Lawrence Lowell, as a corporation sole, has not got into the way of anything else. He has not stopped the emergence of some other and truer idea of a corporation in the same sphere in which he is one. The idea of the king as a corporation sole *has* got into the way of something else. It has stopped the emergence—or rather not stopped, but blurred and confused the emergence—of the great and true idea that all the people of England, as members of one body, including the king their head, and carrying the king on their shoulders with them, are the true and only corporation of England in the sphere of politics. This is not Republicanism (the king is still there as head of the body): it is good old mediæval theory, and it was a theory still known to our lawyers in the sixteenth century. A Chief Justice was declaring in 1522, 'A corporation is an aggregation of head and body: not a head by itself nor a body by itself; and it must be, consonant to reason, for otherwise it is worth naught.' That is good sense; and it is a pity that it was ever forgotten, and that the king became a corporation sole, or 'head by itself'. It caused a good deal of trouble; and it is still causing trouble to-day. When I see the king, in the change lately made in the Coronation Oath, made to speak about 'My possessions', I see that the corporation sole, or head by itself, is still floating about. And I murmur to myself that any possessions, any rights, any duties, in the sphere of our national politics, really appertain and belong to a corporation aggregate, of which you and I are members along with the king our head—not we alone, nor he alone, but all of us together. That is the true political corporation—the true owner of the possessions, rights, and duties common to the people; and if a word is wanted for it, the right word, as Maitland said (and it is a good old sixteenth-century word), is the word Commonwealth. It is a word which has been borrowed for the Empire, to which, I venture to think, it does not really belong. The Empire is not a common-wealth, but a number of allied and kindred common-wealths. And one of these commonwealths is the commonwealth of this island.

It is in the sphere of social life, and in regard to the groups, corporate or unincorporate, which move in that sphere, that Maitland has, I think, taught us most. There is a word or term morphology which Goethe, I believe, introduced into science. It is defined as a branch of biology which is concerned with the form of animals and plants, and with the factors which govern or influence that form. Using that word, I should say that Maitland was a master of social morphology. He studied the forms of society, in mediæval, modern, and contemporary times, and he studied the factors (above all the legal factors) which have governed or influenced, or are governing or influencing, these forms. The great factor which he studied was the English law of Trust. A trust, I may remind you, is in its origin (it begins in 1400 or thereabouts) a legal act by which a landowner, tied by the law of primogeniture,

contrives to release some of his property, and to vest it in
trustees who will hold it in trust, to the use and for the
benefit of his younger sons and his daughters. Very good,
you will say, but what has that got to do with social
morphology or with the growth of societies? Very much,
Maitland will tell us: at any rate in England and so far as
English law is concerned. As the law of Trust develops,
it is found that a growing society can take advantage of it
as easily as the solitary dying landowner. The members
of a society collect subscriptions; they vest them in a
permanent body of trustees, who can always be renewed
by fresh election or by simple co-optation; the trustees
hold the subscriptions, and any other funds of property,
to the use and for the benefit of the society; and lo and
behold, the society is a going concern, with the necessary
buildings, and the necessary general resources, for the
achievement of the common purpose by which it is held
together. The society needs no incorporation, which
might put it at the mercy of the State, since the State
might refuse to grant it: it only needs to 'trustify' itself,
which it can do by going to any lawyer, and when it has
done that it can trust the Lord Chancellor, who sees to
the observance of trusts, to keep the trustees in order. In
this way, as Maitland showed, and showed by a wealth of
examples, the trust has been with us, for the last three or
four hundred years, a great 'instrument of social experimentation'. It has been a dominant factor in the history
of our social morphology. The Free Churches have availed
themselves of it; Trade Unions have availed themselves
of it; commercial and industrial companies have availed
themselves of it; clubs, literary and philosophical societies,

whatever you like, have all availed themselves of it. The
pulsation of social life has caught at a legal instrument,
and used it, 'by kind permission' of the law, for the
achievement of its own objects. That reminds me of a
saying of Maitland, which I think is apposite. 'The one
thing that it is safe to predict is that in England social-
political will take precedence of jurisprudential considerations.' In other words, we let the growth of English
society catch at our law, mould our law, use our law for
its purposes. Blessings on the law which has been so
amenable. Blessings above all on the law of Trust, which
has listened so readily to social persuasion. We owe to it
more than we know.

We owe to it, for example, a great deal of our religious
and what I may call our economic liberty. Where would
Free Churches and Trade Unions have been if it had not
been for our law of Trust? It is difficult to imagine the
answer, or to detect the dim and dusty retreat to which
they might otherwise have been condemned. Wesleyans
owe much to John Wesley: they also owe something to
the Lord Chancellor. It was in firm reliance on the Lord
Chancellor that John Wesley set his seal, in 1784, to a
document declaring the trusts on which he held certain
lands and buildings in various parts of England. That
document secured the Wesleyan Church in the free and
unfettered, yet guaranteed, enjoyment of all its scattered
chapels and their various funds. It is natural for Maitland
to say, reflecting on these facts, 'All that we English people
mean by religious liberty has been intimately connected
with the making of trusts.' If by religious liberty we mean
not merely the liberty of the individual, but the liberty of

the religious society, and if we realise that a religious society, in order to possess liberty, must be free to own and control its buildings and its funds, we shall readily see that religious liberty is closely connected with the law of Trust. The trust was a screen behind which a religious society could lie perdu, in unmolested security; or again, to use another of Maitland's metaphors, it was a back-stair —a blessed wide back-stair—up which religious society could climb to the height of being corporate (or shall I say 'quasi-corporate'? at any rate corporate enough for every practical purpose) without needing to be incorporated.

What protected the Free Churches, and indeed any Church that sought the protection, was ready to protect also the Trade Union. Trade Unions owe much to many brave labour leaders: they also owe something, just like the Wesleyans, to the Lord Chancellor. Nor need we stop at them. The whole general history of our social morphology is intertwined with the trust. 'Behind the screen of trustees, and concealed from the direct scrutiny of legal theories, all manner of groups can flourish: Lincoln's Inn, or Lloyd's, or the Stock Exchange, or the Jockey Club, a whole Presbyterian system, or even the Church of Rome with the Pope at its head.'...'So wide was that blessed back-stair.'

But I must come to an end. If I try to summarise the chief idea, which I want to leave in your minds, I should do so in this way. Sociology runs into law, and is intertwined with the concepts of the lawyers. We should have societies without lawyers; but the forms which societies take are largely dependent on the boxes which lawyers provide for their reception and incubation. Our English law has provided a generous box; and that has helped the germination of our English societies. But the interesting thing about the box which is called Trust is that it was not provided for societies. It was provided, as we have seen, for something else; but the box which the lawyers made for something else was found by societies, and turned by them (of course with the aid and connivance of the lawyers) to another purpose—the purpose of social experimentation. A most interesting thing, as I say; and it leads us on to reflect upon another interesting thing. The Marxists say that the interest of a dominant social class precipitates law, and precipitates it in its own favour. Does it? The story which Maitland tells shows, indeed, that the interest of the feudal landowner originally precipitated the law of Trust; but it also shows another thing —that the law thus precipitated ultimately came to serve a very different and a vastly greater social interest, the interest of little struggling village chapels and of striving and fighting Trade Unions. Now a Marxist would admit that a law once precipitated for one purpose may come incidentally, by acquiring a sort of independent life, to serve other purposes. But will that admission cover the story which Maitland tells? Hardly. A law which in the great range of its application, for the last three or four centuries, has served purposes almost the opposite of those of its origin, at any rate in so far as class-interest is concerned, is a law which cannot be explained by the principle of class-interest. Class-interest may have started it; but it has escaped from the interest which started it, and run magnificently wild. The growth of our English society, the poor as well as the rich, has poured itself into this box of trust. The law of Trust has been impartially accommodating: it has aided equally the growth of different social interests, or, if it has aided any one interest particularly, it has aided particularly the interest of the poor. Anyhow, it has aided, as Maitland says, the general process of social experimentation. That is a great thing, perhaps the greatest of all things, if you believe, as I do, that the process of social experimentation is prior to the State, is greater than the State, and must be served and preserved by the State.

We may therefore thank Maitland, with a deep gratitude, for the light he has shed on the social growth of our people. Perhaps it is also a light on the normal growth of all peoples. Perhaps we may even add that it is a light which should guide future growth. Free social experimentation—in the field of religious life, which cries aloud to-day for such ventures; in the field of economic life, which knows no panacea but demands every experiment of remedy—free social experimentation...what can be greater?